NEW PERSPECTIVES IN SOCIOLOGY

Edited by John Wakeford

This series provides an opportunity for young
sociologists to present original material and also
to summarise and review critically certain key
themes and controversies in their subject. All the
authors are experts in their own field and each
monograph not only provides stimulating ideas for
the specialist but also represents in itself a significant
personal contribution to the discipline.

Students of sociology will find the series invaluable.
For non-specialists the monographs provide a clear
and authoritative insight into the concerns and
perspectives of the modern sociologist.

Other titles in the series

Published

In preparation

Social Order, Reform and Revolution

A power, exchange and institutionalisation perspective

BOB JESSOP

Fellow of Downing College,
Cambridge

Macmillan

© Robert Douglas Jessop 1972

First published 1972 by
THE MACMILLAN PRESS LTD
London and Basingstoke
Associated companies in New York Toronto
Dublin Melbourne Johannesburg and Madras

SBN 333 11541 4

Printed in Great Britain by
A. WHEATON & CO
Exeter

To Lesley

Contents

Preface

In this monograph I present a new perspective in sociological theory and apply it to the analysis of social order, reform and revolution. This perspective is based on a critical examination of three major contemporary sociological approaches to macro-social analysis – consensus theory, conflict theory and exchange theory. In examining these approaches I have been particularly concerned with their emergent themes and joint emphases and with their different advantages and disadvantages for the study of social order. With these criticisms in mind a new analytical framework is presented and a theoretical model is then generated with the aid of several realistic and mutually consistent assumptions. Although this model is based on existing theoretical approaches it goes beyond them in its demonstration of the complexity – even at the most general theoretical level – of the conditions of social order and their variation across types of social structure. I have also illustrated the model through reference to a wide range of cases – extending from primitive band society to historical bureaucratic empires and contemporary Western capitalist societies. The book concludes with a critical appraisal of the model in its present state of development and suggests new lines of empirical research and theoretical inquiry.

The analysis presented in these pages is part of a more extensive project on the nature of sociological theory and its relevance to the analysis of social order, reform and revolution. It is thus very much a presentation of work in progress and, although the basic framework is obviously felt to be fundamentally correct, the precise formulation must necessarily be treated as provisional. I am currently engaged in further developments in the areas outlined in the concluding chapter and hope to publish the results of these investigations at a later date.

The original insight into the significance of exchange theory for the synthesis of consensus and conflict theories was first formulated more than five years ago at the University of Exeter. It has since been developed intermittently as time permitted and particularly under the stimulus of two events. The first of these was the series of seminars and the International Conference on Twentieth-Century Political Revolutions held at King's College, Cambridge, during 1968 and 1969. For these seminars I prepared a number of working papers on theories of social order, reform and revolution as well as papers on Indian Independence and the Kemalist Revolution in Turkey. The second major stimulus behind the present work was the need to formulate a general theoretical framework within which to fit my empirical research on English political culture. An earlier version of this framework was outlined in my paper on 'Exchange and Power in Structural Analysis' in 'Sociological Review' (1969). It is a revised version of this framework that provides the conceptual infrastructure of the present monograph. Further reflections on inherent and emergent contradictions will be found in a paper to be published in 'Social Change', edited by John Jackson and published by the Cambridge University Press, later this year.

Finally I would like to acknowledge several intellectual debts that cannot be adequately reciprocated or expressed in more personal form – those to authors on whose work I have drawn and who have inspired my approach and its formulation. These debts are greatest for those whose views I have examined in the second and third chapters of this book and also for the historical sociology and theoretical work of Samuel Eisenstadt. At the same time I should also like to emphasise that I bear sole responsibility for the analysis that is presented in these pages and for any errors that it may contain.

There is one last debt that I wish to acknowledge – this time of a more personal kind. My wife, Lesley, has given me constant encouragement in this as in other tasks. It is to her that I have dedicated this book.

Cambridge   Bob Jessop
November 1971

1 The Problem of Order

In Londonderry and other places recently, a minority of agitators determined to subvert lawful authority played a part in setting light to highly inflammable material. But the tinder for that fire, in the form of grievance real or imaginary, had been piling up for years. And so I saw it as our duty to do two things. First, to be firm in the maintenance of law and order, and in resisting those elements which seek to profit from any disturbances. Secondly, to ally firmness with fairness, and to look at any underlying causes of dissension which were troubling decent and moderate people. . . . The changes which we have announced are genuine and far-reaching changes and the Government is totally committed to them. I would not preside over an Administration which would water them down or make them meaningless. You will see when the members of the Londonderry Commission are appointed that we intend to live up to our words that this will be a body to command confidence and respect. You will see that in housing allocations we mean business. You will see that legislation to appoint an Ombudsman will be swiftly introduced.[1]

Our only hope was that we would get through to the ordinary people, who hadn't believed in Terence O'Neill's speech, but who didn't see what they could do about it. Our function in marching from Belfast to Derry was to break the truce, to relaunch the civil rights movement as a mass movement, and to show people that O'Neill was, in fact, offering them nothing. . . . The people have made their situation clear. We will fight for justice. We will try to achieve it by peaceful means. But if it becomes necessary we will simply make it impossible for any unjust government to govern us. We will refuse to have anything to do with it. We will build our own houses and refuse to pay rent on those houses to the Government. We will take control of our own areas and we will run them. We'll build our own factories, we'll pay taxes to our own people, and the Government can sit in Stormont and govern whoever [*sic*] will put up with it, for more and more people will stand by a fair system, however illegal, than will stand by a discredited government.[2]

... we have been betrayed by the policies of O'Neill. He takes every opportunity to smear the Protestants, and to eulogise and to condone the actions of the Roman Catholic Church, and her puppet politicians, and her puppet priests, cardinals, monseigneurs, and canons. In pursuit of this treacherous policy of O'Neill there has been the reign and rule of two laws in Ulster. A rigid hard law of blatant injustice to Protestants . . . (and) O'Neill's policy of appeasing popery.[3]

O'Neill has demonstrated quite forcibly that he is neither a Unionist nor a Loyalist. The political game that he is playing is subversive of our well-being. The policy of moderation is the policy of toleration, the policy of toleration is the policy of cowardice, and cowardice is politically suicidal.[4]

These three perspectives on the recent situation in Northern Ireland do not exhaust the range of variation in attitudes and policies towards social order, reform and revolution in that troubled community. They none the less suggest a number of questions about order, reform and revolution. How did their proponents come to hold such views and how accurate are they? More precisely, can the sociologist help us to understand the viewpoints and perspectives of the reformer, the reactionary, the revolutionary? Can he help us to discriminate and evaluate the differing stands and conflicting actions of the protagonists in such a conflict? What are the social factors underlying individual and collective dissent in such a situation? What factors determine the relative success or failure of the different antagonists in maintaining or reorganising the distribution of power and rewards? How inevitable are such conflicts and how inevitable are their outcomes? To what extent is the conflict in Northern Ireland comparable with conflicts at other times and places? To what extent is a general theory of social order, reform and revolution possible and what would it look like? Does the social scientist interested in order and change have a social responsibility to help or to hinder the maintenance of order, the promotion of reform, the advancement of revolution? It is with these and similar questions that we shall be concerned in the following pages. We begin our discussion with a consideration of the last two questions – the nature of a theory of social order and the nature of the social responsibility of the sociologist. In succeeding chapters we shall examine some divergent theoretical approaches to the study of order, reform and revolution and suggest some points of convergence; elaborate and illustrate a general model of order and change; and finally we shall mention some areas for further investigation and theoretical endeavour. We turn first, however, to some comments on sociological theory and the general nature of order, reform and revolution.

Theory in Sociology

This monograph is concerned primarily with the development of a general theory of social order, reform and revolution. It is thus comparative and macrosocial in orientation. Theory involves more than a single hypothesis or lawlike generalisation (e.g. if x, then y). It involves a systematically related set of statements, including some lawlike generalisations, that is empirically testable.[5] Any simple hypothesis or lawlike statement implies a more complex theoretical model and the process of theory-building involves both the explication of the concepts, assumptions and perspectives that are implicit in the hypothesis and also their articulation into some formal logical structure from which the original hypothesis can be derived.[6] The greater the number of such hypotheses and the wider their implications, the more parsimonious their formulation and the more precise their predictions, then the stronger the theory.[7]

The basis for their articulation, the rationale for theory construction, can be variously derived. It may come from analogy with models for the investigation of other phenomena, from examination of the phenomena themselves and the abstraction of relations between them, and/or from the assumptions and conceptual connections of the theory itself.[8] The last approach has several distinct advantages – advantages with both a general and an immediate theoretical relevance. Generally, such 'symbolic theory' is the most formal in its construction and thus more readily subject to empirical evaluation. The rationale derives from conceptual definition and interconnection and from rationally consistent assumptions[9] and the model is thus able to provide a more determinate and flexible mechanism for the generation of hypotheses and explanations. Because the rationale is conceptual it is also more amenable to manipulation and refinement

3

in order to ensure greater precision in prediction – especially for cases outside the realm of immediate experimental observation. Finally symbolic theory should also provide a greater understanding of the relations between variables than mere extrapolation or more rigid analogies.[10]

The general advantages of this approach can be illustrated by a comparison of the methods of abstraction and symbolic interconnection in the development of theories of revolution.[11] The abstractive method of theory construction produces models dependent for their validity on accurate abstractions from historical events *and* on the abstraction of relevant events. However, such models have no explicit criterion of relevance other than regularity – an event or class of events is probably causal if it occurs in almost every instance of revolution studied and is absent in instances of not-revolution. Moreover, abstraction often proceeds with an inadequately defined theoretical universe so that comparisons are made between incomparable phenomena and more relevant phenomena are excluded from consideration.[12] The result is all too often inconsistency and contradiction across the models: the factors held to be causally significant in the French revolution, for example, range

from the intellectual (inadequate political socialisation, conflicting social myths, corrosive social philosophy, alienation of intellectuals) to economic (increasing poverty, rapid growth, imbalance of production and distribution, long-term growth plus short-term recession) to social (resentment due to restricted élite circulation, confusion due to excessive élite recruitment, anomie due to excessive social mobility or social stagnation, conflict due to the rise of new classes) to the political (bad government, divided government, weak government, oppressive government).[13]

Moreover, the result is frequently evidential rather than explanatory – providing descriptions of revolutionary situations rather than explanations of revolution. Finally the explanations, in so far as they are presented, are often weak and implausible.[14]

Conversely, a well-constructed symbolic model avoids these problems. Firstly, the criterion of relevance is given in the concepts and their interrelations; and these also provide for the deduction of testable hypotheses rather than their empirical abstraction. Secondly, the model provides a taxonomy of revolu-

4

tions thereby permitting the search for (as well as suggesting) causes specific to theoretically meaningful subclasses of revolution. The abstracted model looks for events common to all revolutions or has recourse to *ad hoc* subclassifications. Thirdly, the symbolic model provides explanations rather than simple descriptions. These explanations are also typically strong and plausible – being derived from a set of rationally consistent assumptions and meaningfully interconnected concepts. Finally the usefulness of a theory may be traced back to its rationale and this is not given in the data but imposed on them; such imposition is best attained through interpretive, imaginative application of conceptual schemes and assumptions rather than through an undirected examination of the data.

There is also a more immediate (and quite separate) reason for adopting a symbolic strategy in constructing our general theory of order, reform and revolution. This monograph is primarily concerned with the convergence of different sociological theories and such a task almost inevitably proceeds from an examination of the interrelations and connections, the assumptions and assertions, the perspectives and values, of the different theories and then turns to an attempt at their integration through combination, redefinition, conceptual connection and assumption. Some of this conceptual elaboration will involve the transformation of categorical and polar concepts into variables, some will involve the decomposition of compound concepts into their constituent elements, some will involve establishing equivalencies between apparently different concepts, some will involve establishing contingent or variant relations between different concepts, and some will involve the modification of assumptions and the specification of their respective spheres of relevance.[15] In short a symbolic approach is more or less implicit in the task before us; and formalisation rather than verification must be the primary concern. The confrontation of different theories with empirical data can lead to the rejection of one or more theories and/or point to the need for debate and synthesis. It cannot in itself provide such a unification.[16] The actual task of theory construction must depend in this case on the development and application of a theory – although it is clear that such a theory must be testable and should not directly contradict what is already 'precisely known' about order, reform and revolution.[17] Accordingly we shall first introduce a sociologically meaningful definition of these three concepts as a preliminary rationale for our theoretical investigations and then proceed to an examination of different approaches to these phenomena as a basis for synthesis and theory formation.

Social Order

Social order is a variable property of societies. It exists to the extent that there is peaceful coexistence in the operation of social institutions. These institutions may be violent or non-violent. Indeed all orderly societies contain institutions that are inherently violent and in some societies order depends on the systematic and regular employment of violence.[18] Likewise these institutions may be conflictual or non-conflictual. Every society has institutionalised mechanisms of conflict resolution although these certainly vary in terms of recognised methods and matters of contention. All that order requires is acceptance of the institutional structure of the society in question. This acceptance may be pragmatic or normative provided it results in peaceful coexistence or the absence of uninstitutionalised conflict. Recognition of economic interests and submission to *force majeure*, as well as value commitments, can lead to acquiescence in the established social and cultural system.[19] A modicum of consensus is therefore necessary to social order but it need not be extensive in scope, intensive in character, uniform in distribution, nor normative in origin. Moreover, as we shall demonstrate later, the significance of normative consensus for social order varies inversely with the degree of structural differentiation in society and the hierarchisation of power. In short, an emphasis on consensus in the definition of order can be misleading and we prefer to leave open, at least for the moment, the question of the preconditions of peaceful coexistence.

Social order is not only compatible with violence and conflict; it is also compatible with social change. Indeed the stability of social order may well depend on continuing reorganisation of established institutions and also on institutional innovation. But equally social change may itself contribute to a breakdown in the peaceful coexistence of social order. The conditions under which social change facilitates or hinders the maintenance of order must therefore be examined if we are to develop a general theory of social order, reform and revolution.

Reform and Revolution

Reform and revolution are both types of social change. They have been variously distinguished. Some writers have argued that it is the content of their belief systems that distinguishes reformist from revolutionary movements and thus reform from revolution. The more radical the beliefs and proposed changes, the more rapid their projected implementation or realisation, the more general their scope – the more revolutionary the movement.[20] Others have argued that it is the means used to implement or promote the beliefs and proposals that is the distinguishing characteristic. Typically the criterion is the use or threatened use of violence; occasionally it is the legality or illegality of the methods used.[21] Others again have merely emphasised the suddenness of the changes effected by the movement in question.[22]

While all three distinctions are relevant and useful in the comparative analysis of social movements and social change, they seem to us to focus on contingent rather than necessary features of reform and revolution. For reform and revolution as types of social change can have no sociological meaning outside the socio-cultural context in which they occur. The degree of radicalism or the methods employed do not in themselves make a movement reformist or revolutionary. The defining characteristic is the relationship between these methods or a given degree of radicalism and the attitudes of the powerful in society. Thus a simple emphasis on violent or illegal means ignores the extent to which violence is institutionalised in society[23] and to which the legal system is a dead letter; while an emphasis on radicalism ignores the extent to which the social definition of the revolutionary depends simply on the admissibility of the projected changes (whether or not radical) into the dominant value system of the society in question.[24] The key feature of a revolutionary movement is therefore the fact of its derogation or proscription by the powerful, whereas a reformist movement is one preferred or prescribed by the powerful. Radicalism and violence can thus be seen as contingent aspects of revolutionary movements : these qualities are often, but not invariably, derogated while even non-violent and non-radical movements can be proscribed as revolutionary or subversive. In short, revolutionary and reformist movements can be defined in terms of their level of institutionalisation and then compared in terms of their radicalism and methods. Reform and revolution can in turn be distinguished in terms of their origins in, and implementation by, one or other type of movement.

This emphasis upon the sociological fact of institutionalisation or its absence in the definition of reform and revolution can be justified on both theoretical and empirical grounds. The idea of institutionalisation has been a central concern of sociologists for many years and thus the present emphasis not only provides a clear rationale but also enables us to articulate our analysis of reform and revolution with more general theoretical work in sociology. Moreover, there are demonstrable *qualitative* differences between movements that are institutionalised and those that are not. The impact of variations in the level of institutionalisation can be seen in the strategy and dynamics of similar movements in different societies and of different movements within the same society. Processes of bureaucratisation and goal displacement, for example, are less likely to occur in radical movements that are proscribed than those that are permitted.[25] Similarly movements that are originally non-radical may become increasingly radical and violent if proscribed and thus come to attack the whole society rather than a limited aspect.[26] If such an escalation of dissent is then followed by a relaxation of proscription, the potential for far-reaching revolution will have been much increased.[27] Moreover, in a structurally differentiated society, the existence of support from one or more power centres for an otherwise derogated or proscribed movement may well facilitate successful implementation of its programme of social change – especially if that support comes from the military.[28] A more rigorous and extensive study of the nature, ramifications and influence of variation in the level of institutionalisation is clearly required; but attention must also be paid to the other factors that determine the degree of radicalism and the type of methods employed by different movements in the promotion of social change. All three problems will be examined in more detail below during the course of theory construction.

Social Order, Social Theory and the Value-Problem

The value-problem is omnipresent in sociological analysis but it is particularly acute when one deals with controversial phenomena such as revolution. There are actually several aspects to the value-problem and they impinge on different stages of the

8

research process. Some are more problematic than others and each demands some consideration.

Firstly, there is the question of the connection between one's values and the choice of subject for investigation. Is a revolutionary, for example, disqualified from studying revolution because of his commitment to the promotion of revolution? Or does that commitment make him better qualified to conduct research? The answer to both questions must be no. The choice of subject belongs to the 'antechamber of science' and has no necessary connection with the scientific validity of subsequent research.[29]

Secondly, there is the related question of the choice of a perspective in the analysis of the chosen area of investigation. This is more problematic. Some have argued that this is again unimportant – belonging as it does to the antechamber of science. Rigorous application of scientific method and caution in generalising from the necessarily limited results of one's work ensure that values do not influence empirical investigation and theoretical evaluation.[30] Opposed to this viewpoint is the argument that causal analysis involves valuation through the selection of particular causes from the multiplicity of different causes producing a class of events and that the scientific method itself cannot be value-free. The length of causal chains, the relative specificity of selected causes, the possible neglect of by-products and side-effects of given causes, and the very multiplicity of such causes – all these imply that causal explanation involves valuation and thus has ideological implications.[31] Moreover, in so far as any theoretical model provides only a limited perspective and there remains a disjunction between theoretical concepts and operational definitions, the mere process of classification and the subsumption of given phenomena under one's theoretical universe involves valuation.[32] In addition the critera adopted for acceptance or rejection of the theoretical model and its explicit hypotheses may be more or less rigorous and thus open to value-influences.[33] In short, the antagonists of value-freedom argue that the scientific method itself is open to value-bias and its application to value-imbued theories is not a sufficient condition for their neutralisation.

Such criticism cannot be ignored but much of it is misdirected at the scientific method itself rather than at individual sociologists and at the hasty generalisation of results. Adherence to specified rules of procedure can minimise much of this value-bias; although it cannot eliminate it. The more explicit the theoretical and operational definitions, the more advanced the levels of measurement, the more varied and diverse the hypotheses to be tested, the greater the emphasis on critical tests rather than cumulation of positive cases, the more rigorous the criteria for acceptance, and so forth, the less the risk of value-bias. But the perspective of the investigator will necessarily survive the scientific method and imbue the presentation of theory and hypothesis; this is inevitable since any statement at all about reality must be a statement in terms of some conceptual scheme rather than another and the choice of conceptual scheme is value-relevant.[34] In short, while the protagonists of a value-free sociology are right in arguing that a self-consciously exacting application of scientific method will reduce value-bias, the antagonists are right in arguing that it is impossible to eliminate such bias. None the less the possibility of constricting the scope of ideological influence can be pursued and should be pursued in so far as one is interested in the advancement of understanding and prediction rather than the promotion of particular theories.

Thirdly there is the problem of 'ideological distortion' or the overextension of one's findings in so far as they are verified by rigorous empirical analysis.[35] This problem is particularly relevant to the length of causal chains involved in the theoretical formulations and also to the general multiplicity of causes. Greater modesty on the part of investigators could do much to reduce such distortions; and, since such distortions result in bad scientific statements, they can also be eliminated by further investigation.[36]

Finally there is the problem of the social responsibility of the social scientist and the question of explicit value-judgement by the social scientist. Value-judgement on a scientific basis would be possible only if there were a single valid rational ethic, that is, a set of values which can be rationally defended as holding good for all men at all times.[37] Logically, however, it is impossible to derive a moral conclusion from a set of non-moral premises and it is therefore impossible for the sociologist to derive *from sociological study alone* any conclusions as to the morality or immorality of individual and collective actions. Such study is none the less relevant to moral evalution. Firstly it can undermine the moral justification of certain actions by showing, let us say, that a given action does not have the effects which are invoked in its justification. Secondly it can perhaps be employed to establish criteria of one kind or another which can be overridden only by reference to particularly important values.[38] Thus Sklar argues that it is possible to establish the nature of a society in which men have no complaints against their social institutions and that such a society would be a good yardstick for the evaluation of existing societies.[39] Such a yardstick can certainly be overridden by an appeal to values other than that men should have no complaints against their social institutions – by appeal, for example, to the role of suffering in the attainment of spiritual salvation[40] – but it does provide a reasonably defensible value position. Unfortunately it is apparently impossible to provide an unambiguous description of the structure of such a society : the nearest one gets to such descriptions are generalisations of the kind :

> First, each person engaged in an institution or affected by it has an equal right to the most extensive liberty compatible with a like liberty for all; and second, inequalities as defined by the institutional structure or fostered by it are arbitrary unless it is reasonable to expect that they will work out to everyone's advantage and provided that the positions and offices to which they attach may be gained and are open to all.[41]

> In the distribution of rewards, priority should be given to need over merit and contribution to the common good . . .[42] free inequality of praise, no inequality of respect . . . in a just society inequalities of status would only be defensible where they could plausibly be shown to be inequalities of praise.[43]

Quite clearly principles such as these cannot yield unambiguous statements as to the moral propriety of specific inequalities – indeed there are many distributions which can be generated by just institutions and an apparently just distribution which has not been so generated cannot be considered just in terms of this particular criterion.[44] None the less such principles can be employed to make broad discriminations between societies provided that we realise that their application involves value-judgements capable of being undermined or overridden and not the specification of a rational sociological ethic.

Our own commitment is indeed to the society in which men have no complaints against their social institutions and we shall employ it as a yardstick in analysing different societies and social movements. The sociologist is not disqualified from making such

11

value-judgements nor from undermining those of others; but he is no less liable to have his judgements overridden and undermined. Moreover, in so far as he is committed to the advancement of understanding and prediction, the sociologist should maintain the distinction between fact and value-judgement and refrain from allowing his values to affect the scientific status of his work. Since the primary aim of the present work is the advancement of theoretical understanding of social order and change, we shall be happy to have our own work assessed in terms of such a criterion.

In short the process of sociological study can be relatively value-free provided that sociologists adhere to rigorous scientific methods of analysis. Sociological study is none the less relevant to moral evaluation. The results of such study can undermine value-positions and can also be employed to facilitate or to hinder the achievement of various values. The sociologist is thus in a position to discriminate among the different actions of the antagonists in a potentially revolutionary situation and also to help directly or indirectly one or more of the parties to such a conflict. But there is nothing inherent in sociological study itself that will enable him to determine those questions without resort to value-judgement. The moral responsibility of the sociologist thus becomes increasingly acute as his research approaches fruition and its social consequences are as yet undetermined. The least he can do at this point is to examine the possible value-implications of that research and to clarify his own value-positions on these implications. He may also feel it necessary to publicise such implications and value-judgements and to attempt to realise those consequences of which he approves.[45]

Summary and Conclusions

In this chapter we have been primarily concerned with setting the present monograph in its theoretical and moral context. This monograph is concerned with the development of a general theory of social order, reform and revolution and we have argued in favour of a 'symbolic' approach to theory construction. Symbolic theory is more formal in construction, has a more determinate and flexible mechanism for hypothesis generation, is more amenable to manipulation and refinement, is able to provide a greater understanding of the relations between variables. Moreover, a symbolic approach is more or less implied in our current interest in the convergence of different sociological theories of order and change. Within this context we outlined a conceptual scheme for the analysis of order, reform and revolution based on the notion of institutionalisation. This will provide the rationale for constructing the general theory in later chapters. Finally, we examined the value-problem in sociological analysis from several aspects and concluded that, while sociology itself can be relatively value-free, the sociologist himself has a moral responsibility for the consequences of his research. In this second context we stated our own commitment to the idea of justice as fairness in the analysis of social institutions and the evaluation of different social movements. The consequences of both these decisions should become apparent as we proceed with the construction of our general theory of social order, reform and revolution.

2 Approaches to the Study of Order

Social order exists to the extent that there is peaceful coexistence in the operation of social institutions. The existence of social order is a fundamental problem for sociological theory. For it is inherent in social life that the actions of one individual (or group) can facilitate or hinder those of another individual (or group). Thus in every social situation there is a latent tension as to whether one or more of the actors will in fact behave – intentionally or unintentionally – so as to facilitate or hinder the actions of another. This tension may manifest itself in a conflict between actors for control over the actions of others to ensure their co-operation in the attainment of goals determined by those who emerge successfully from that conflict. Such a conflict may lead to an unlimited struggle for domination in which all possibility of attaining other goals is lost and many scarce resources are expended. The extent to which such a latent tension is manifested depends on the particular social situation rather than on the general form assumed by the problem of order. While the contingency of order is indeed grounded ultimately in the nature of interaction itself, the particular structure of a concrete interactive situation is the immediate determinant of that contingency and the extent and manner of its realisation. Likewise the resolution of the problem of order will vary from situation to situation. Social order is possible only through the regulation of interaction among individuals and groups to prevent unlimited struggle and to confine conflict to institutionalised modes of contention. But the manner and mode of such regulation will obviously vary according to the particular structure of the concrete interactive situation and the particular tensions implied by that structure. We should therefore be concerned with the development of a theory that allows for various modes of resolving the problem of order rather than with one that posits a single unique solution. This monograph is concerned with just such a task.

Quite clearly formulation of the problem of social order in these terms in no way commits one to the normative solution posited by consensus theorists. It also disqualifies the solution proposed by some conflict theorists which rests on the elimination of conflict through the overthrow of class structures : the problem of order is inherent in social life and cannot be resolved simply through the elimination of particular conflicts. The problem of order is more intractable than has been assumed by most contemporary sociological theorists and it must be re-examined in the light of the present formulation. In this chapter therefore we shall examine different approaches to the study of order and attempt to state the various advantages and disadvantages they possess for the theoretical analysis of order, reform and revolution. We begin this examination with a consideration of normative functionalism and then turn to conflict and exchange theories.

Normative Functionalism

Normative functionalist theories[1] are concerned primarily with the normative regulation of interaction to ensure social order[2] and the continued fulfilment of the functional problems of social systems. The three major points of reference in their analyses are the existence of a shared value system, the four functional problems of any social system, and the interchanges between differentiated social subsystems. All other problems are considered in the light of these three points of reference and especially in the light of values held in common by all members of a given social system.

While the primary concern of normative functionalist theories is indeed the normative regulation of interaction to ensure social order, the most general concern is the analytical study of social action—the structures and processes whereby meaningful intentions are formed and more or less successfully implemented in behaviour.[3] It is within this more general context that their contributions to the study of social order must be evaluated. Action is analysed in terms of its four subsystems. These are the cultural, the social, the psychological, and the organismic systems.[4] The cultural subsystem comprises the meanings and intentions of action that are shared by the members of the total action system. The social subsystem comprises the normatively patterned interaction of these members. The personality subsystem refers to the need-dispositions and orientations of individual actors in the total system of action. And the organismic subsystem consists simply

15

in the species-type which sets limits to the possibilities of action and provides the basic energy for such action. These four subsystems are analytically distinct but they are empirically interpenetrating. A general theory of action clearly requires, therefore, the development of laws and hypotheses not only about the internal structure and processes of each subsystem but also about the interrelations between different subsystems. Normative functionalist theories posit an essential homology of structure and function in each of these four subsystems and in the total system of action such that, for example, each is confronted with the same four functional problems, each is characterised by four generalised media of exchange between their respective functional subsystems, and each subsystem of action is characterised by a specific function within the total system of action.[5] In the present context, however, we are concerned only with the analysis of the social system and its articulation with other systems and not with a detailed consideration of all four subsystems of action and their relations with each other, with the physical environment, and with ultimate reality.[6] To the examination of social systems we now turn.

Every social system is confronted with four functional problems. These problems are those of pattern maintenance, integration, goal-attainment, and adaptation. Pattern-maintenance refers to the need to maintain and reinforce the basic values of the social system and to resolve tensions that emerge from continuing commitment to these values. Integration refers to the allocation of rights and obligations, rewards and facilities, to ensure the harmony of relations between members of the social system. Goal attainment involves the necessity of mobilising actors and resources in organised ways for the attainment of specific goals. And adaptation refers to the need for the production or acquisition of generalised facilities or resources that can be employed in the attainment of various specific goals. Social systems tend to differentiate about these problems so as to increase the functional capabilities of the system. Such differentiation – whether through the temporal specialisation of a structurally undifferentiated unit or through the emergence of two or more structurally distinct units from one undifferentiated unit – is held to constitute a major verification of the fourfold functionalist schema. It also provides the framework within which are examined the plural interchanges that occur between structurally differentiated units to provide them with the inputs they require in the performance

16

of their functions and to enable them to dispose of the outputs they produce.

Social order depends on the continuing fulfilment of the four functional problems and also on the maintenance of balanced relations between the social system, the other systems of action and the physical environment. Failure to meet these requirements will lead to disturbances in the operation of social institutions and, in the absence of successful resolution of these disturbances so as to ensure continuing conformity to institutionalised role expectations, to social change. Social change is always change in the normative culture of the social system[7] and can vary in degree from structural differentiation within an otherwise stable system to the dissolution of the system as such or its complete change through charismatic innovation.[8] The extent of these disturbances and the degree of social change are contingent on a wide variety of factors and are to a considerable degree theoretically indeterminate.[9] In the following paragraphs we examine the theories of disturbance, differentiation and change propounded by the normative functionalists.

Social change originates in disturbances in the operation of social institutions. These disturbances derive from imbalances in the relation between the social system and its environments and/ or from imbalances in the relation between two or more units within the social system.[10] These imbalances (whether consisting in deficient or excessive inputs or outputs in the interchange between the various systems and subsystems of action) constitute a strain towards the modification of the relationship beyond limits compatible with the continuing equilibrium of the social system.[11] There are four main types of endogenous social strain – these types corresponding to the four functional problems outlined above. Value strain poses the issue of commitment to the basic values of the system itself. Normative strain involves imbalances in the integration of the social system. Strain on mobilisation concerns the relationship between activity on behalf of the collectivity and the rewards of that activity. And strain on facilities involves the inadequacy of knowledge, skills and resources for the attainment of various goals.[12] These strains manifest themselves in lowered performance at both the social and the personal level – in failure to achieve collective goals and in symptoms of personal disturbance such as anxiety, phantasy and unsocialised aggression.[13] The symptoms of personal disturbance, especially where they lead to uninstitutionalised attempts at the

17

restructuring of the social system, will be more or less effectively handled and channelled by agencies for social control. Constructive and responsible attempts at social reorganisation will be encouraged, however, and may result in structural differentiation and improved collective performance. We now turn to a more detailed consideration of the normative functionalist theories of institutionalised and uninstitutionalised attempts at social reconstruction and the resolution of social strain.

Collective behaviour has been defined as 'an uninstitutionalised mobilisation for action in order to modify one or more kinds of strain on the basis of a generalised reconstitution of a component of action'.[14] This mobilisation for action is termed uninstitutionalised because it is oriented to situations which are normatively unstructured or undefined and *not* because it is derogated or proscribed by the societal centre.[15] The basis of mobilisation is a belief that posits extraordinary forces at work in the world, that assumes extraordinary consequences following on successful reorganisation of the social system, and that fails to specify in sufficient detail how the system must be reorganised to achieve such consequences.[16] Smelser distinguishes between types of collective behaviour in terms of the content of their generalised beliefs. His five types of uninstitutionalised mobilisation are the panic, the craze, the hostile outburst, the norm-oriented movement and the value-oriented movement. While the panic involves only a flight from the situation of action on the basis of an hysterical belief, the other types of collective behaviour involve the reorganisation of different levels of the system—respectively facilities, roles and collectivities, norms and values.[17] The level of collective behaviour in any given situation is contingent upon many factors and cannot be reduced simply to the level of social strain.

The preconditions of a collective mobilisation are held to be sixfold. The structure of the social system must be conducive to the emergence of the type of mobilisation in question. There must be social strains in the system. There must emerge and spread a generalised belief or belief system that identifies the source of strain, attributes certain characteristics to this source, and also specifies certain responses to the strain as appropriate and possible. While the relationship between social strain and generalised belief is theoretically indeterminate, there is a tendency for the level of collective behaviour to depend on both the seriousness of the initial conditions of strain and the inadequacy

18

of existing facilities at each level of generality to meet the conditions of the strain.[18] There must also be precipitating factors and, fifthly, the actual mobilisation of the participants for action. Finally, there must be ineffective operation of social control before and immediately after the collective action.[19] All six conditions must be present before collective behaviour occurs but there is no necessary sequence in which the conditions must emerge and combine. The development of collective behaviour involves a value-added process in which, although there is a definite temporal sequence of activation, any or all of the determinants may have existed for an indefinite period before activation.[20]

In the present context three classes of collective behaviour are particularly relevant. The panic is clearly not a social movement in the sense of a movement oriented to the implementation of social change;[21] while the craze is relevant only in so far as some social movements are oriented primarily to maintaining or changing the distribution of facilities rather than to the reorganisation of roles, norms and institutions, or values. The hostile outburst, the norm-oriented movement and the value-oriented movement are more pertinent to the analysis of reform and revolution. The hostile outburst is a collective mobilisation on the basis of a generalised aggression against agents held to be responsible for an anxiety-producing strain. Such outbursts can vary in the intensity of their aggression and in the degree of their organisation. Norm-oriented movements attempt to change social structure not simply through the replacement or punishment of role-occupants but also through the modification, revival, creation or protection of norms in the name of a generalised belief. Value-oriented movements are more radical and attempt to restore, protect, modify or create values. Many different sorts of social movement are subsumed under these three categories and we now examine their preconditions in more detail.

Hostile outbursts include race riots, palace coups, slave insurrections, feudal revolts and jacqueries, military coups oriented to the replacement of political leaders without additional structural change, and McCarthyite attacks on suspected subversives. The degree of structural conduciveness is held to depend on three main variables – the structure of responsibility, the availability of alternative channels of protest and the availability of means of spreading hostile beliefs. Hostile outbursts are particularly likely to occur where there is a structure of diffuse responsibility

19

and/or where there are institutionalised scapegoats. Both the strains and the precipitants leading to such outbursts can be many and varied. The nature of the outburst will vary with the degree of leadership and its organisation. Social control varies in its effectiveness according to the ability of the authorities to control communications, to prevent interaction between leaders and followers, to open up alternative channels of protest, to employ repression consistently and to maintain impartiality towards the antagonists in the outburst. The indeterminacy of social structure and collective outburst should be apparent from this account and most of these factors are operative for higher level movements.

Norm-oriented movements include such phenomena as the Know-Nothing Movement, the desegregration movement, female suffragists, anti-slavery campaigners, the Committee of 100 and most pressure groups and military coups. The two major conditions conducive to norm-oriented movements are the possibility of appearing to demand normative or institutional change without challenging values and the availability of access to means of changing norms. Conversely, value-oriented movements (e.g. communism, fascism, millenarianism, pacifism, agrarian socialism) are encouraged by situations in which it is impossible to challenge norms without appearing to challenge the central value system and in which access to means of expressing hostility and implementing normative change is limited.[22] For both types of movement, and especially for value-oriented movements, the strains are multiple and complex and the precipitants are decidedly indeterminate. Charismatic leadership is particularly important in the creation of generalised beliefs and the mobilisation of value-oriented movements; for such leadership is most conducive to those diffuse and total commitments necessary for successful implementation of value change. Social control is also significant in the dynamics of such high-level movements. Depending on the responses of social control agencies a value-oriented movement could develop into an underground conspiracy, a reformist party, a passive cult, a sect or denomination, or a revolutionary movement. The analysis of such movements must therefore consider the whole array of variables and their interrelations if it is to understand the complexities of their structure and dynamics.

Collective behaviour is generally handled and channelled by the public authorities with sufficient effectiveness to ensure that

20

the social system is neither radically dissolved nor radically changed. Radical dissolution is likely only where there are high-level multiple strains and low levels of resources to facilitate mobilisation for reform or revolution. The radical overthrow of the system will occur only where there are high-level multiple strains and a value-oriented movement outside the 'government-and-control apparatus'[23] that is able to mobilise sufficient numbers on the basis of an appropriate ideology to topple the ineffectual existing government and reverse the trends toward decline or, where the government had been successfully introducing social change, to continue the process of development. Where neither dissolution into localism nor revolutionary convulsion and progress occur, long-term development on a continuous or discontinuous basis is likely where the government-and-control apparatus can channel collective behaviour into constructive institutional innovation.[24] The most important variable in determining the long-term direction of change is held to be the activities of the government-and-control apparatus – its planning, its ability to mobilise people and resources in periods of strain, its ability to contain and to respond to protest, and its ability to guide and control institutional innovations.[25]

One type of institutional innovation that has received particular attention from normative functionalists is structural differentiation. Where the social strains productive of collective behaviour are those of a multifunctional unit, the authorities may encourage the resolution of strain through the differentiation of the unit into two or more specialised functional units. Constructive ideas and possible models will be specified and implemented on an experimental basis. Those that are able to overcome the inevitable resistance of institutionalised structures (vested interests) and prove to be effective will become routinised and institutionalised. Successful differentiation involves change at all four levels of social structure. Facilities that were previously ascribed to the undifferentiated or less differentiated unit must be freed for utilisation by the newly differentiated structures. New roles and collectivities will emerge and their structure and organisation must be specified. The integrative subsystem must be restructured to permit the incorporation of the newly differentiated units into full membership of the more general societal community. The value system must be extended and reformulated at a higher level of generality to legitimise the new structures and to provide standards of competence and the like.

Structural differentiation increases the functional capabilities of the system but it also increases the vulnerability of the system to future strains through impairments in the new units and/or their interchanges. Indeed the ramifications of processes of structural differentiation may contribute to the complex and multiple strains that are associated with revolutionary convulsions.[26] It is to the analysis of some of these ramifications that we now turn.

The differentiation of the social system creates new problems for system integration and the maintenance of social order. Each of the differentiated subsystems requires certain factor inputs if it is to perform its own function adequately and each must dispose of its product if the other subsystems are to function in turn. It is inherent in the interchange process that an imbalance may emerge in the acquisition of inputs and the disposition of outputs and so create social strains. An additional complication is introduced by the dependence of highly differentiated societies upon generalised media of exchange for the adequate functioning of the interchanges between subsystems. In such societies the complexity of the interchange process precludes the mediation of input-output transactions by barter or ascriptive obligation or, indeed, centralised administrative direction. Extensive differentiation is thus dependent upon the development of more generalised media to facilitate and sustain the necessary exchanges. At the most general analytical level the normative functionalists posit four such media of exchange – money, power, influence and commitments. Each of these media is generated by one of the four functional subsystems. The adaptive subsystem (or economy) produces money; the goal-attainment subsystem (or polity) produces power; the integrative subsystem (or societal community) generates influence; and the pattern-maintenance subsystem (or cultural system) generates commitments. These generalised media are *symbolic* media and are dependent upon the institutionalisation of a normative framework that regulates their use in exchanges. Consensus on this normative framework and confidence in the continuing worth of the media are therefore particularly important in the maintenance of stability and order in complex societies. A failure to maintain such consensus and confidence is likely to encourage inflationary and deflationary cycles, including certain kinds of craze (e.g. speculative booms, political bandwagons, fashion cycles and religious revivals).[27]

Money is defined in this context as 'the unit's capacity, through

22

market channels under given rules of procedure, to command goods and services in exchange, which for its own reasons it (the acting unit) desires'.[28] Similarly power is seen as a 'generalised capacity to secure the performance of binding obligations by units in a system of collective organisation when the obligations are legitimised with reference to their bearing on collective goals and where in case of recalcitrance there is a presumption of enforcement by negative situational sanctions – whatever the actual agency of that enforcement'.[29] Influence works through support systems and refers to 'the generalised capacity to persuade through the offer of contingent acceptance'.[30] Fourthly, generalised commitments involve 'the capacity through appeal to a subjective sense of obligation to motivate fulfilment of relevant obligations without reference to any threat of situational sanctions (thus differentiating it from power)'.[31] Such generalised commitments mediate interchanges through confidence that others will implement their obligations in the realisation of an individual's or a group's goals and that they in turn will implement their obligations in the realisation of yet others' goals. It would thus seem to involve primarily a norm of indirect reciprocity.

The four media are the symbolic modes of constraint within a more general categorisation of types of sanction. The Parsonian schema distinguishes between (a) the situational and intentional channels of constraint, and (b) the positive and negative modes of constraint. Cross-classification thus produces four types of sanction. Positive-situational sanctions or *inducements* operate through the offer of positive situational advantages for co-operation. Negative-situational sanctions or *coercion* operate through the threat of situational disadvantages from non-compliance. Positive-intentional sanctions or *persuasion* operates through the offer of good reasons why it would, from alter's point of view and independent of situational advantages, 'be a good thing' for him to act as ego wishes. Lastly negative-intentional sanctions or the *activation of commitments* involve attempts to secure co-operation through the offer of good reasons why it would, from alter's own point of view and independent of situational disadvantages, be 'wrong' for him to refuse compliance.[32] It should be clear that the corresponding types of symbolic sanctions are money, power, influence and generalised commitments.

The critical significance of the symbolic media in the Parsonian schema is that they enable the zero-sum condition (i.e. the fixed nature of the stock of sanctions) to be broken by effecting a net addition to the amount of power in the system. The most obvious illustration of this process is the creation of credit in the economy through the operation of the banking mechanism. Not only do banks lend out money deposited by others but they also contribute to an increase in the stock of money by lending out more than has been placed on deposit. The creation of credit in this way means that the monetary system is 'insolvent' at any given moment in time for not all commitments can be met at once – even where formally valid claims to payment exist. This situation is resolved by the use of credit for increasing production. Since money is a symbol and represents in the last resort command over goods and services, the supply of real money can be increased only through an increase in the supply of goods and services. Where the latter fail to materialise inflation is the necessary result. Conversely, where there is an overproduction of goods and services for the market and/or creditors withdraw their investments and hold money or, preferably, gold, then a deflationary cycle begins. Important parallels are held to exist in the operation of the other functional subsystems.

Thus leaders in a democratic and pluralistic political system acquire the freedom to make certain types of binding decisions beyond their mandate and beyond their ability to implement them immediately. Provided that these additional obligations result in the attainment of additional collective goals in the longer run, then the zero-sum constraint on power can be broken. Failure to attain these goals signifies a decrease in the effectiveness of a leader's power and thus the need for greater support to maintain policy outputs. Conversely, the withdrawal of political support or insistence on the immediate implementation of policy decisions will be countered by attempts on the part of leaders to maintain control over such support and to establish a rigid system of priorities for policy implementation. A deflationary cycle marked by an increasing resort to physical coercion will result.[33]

Similarly, in the societal community, officials of voluntary associations can lend the name of their association to encourage particular 'causes' without prior consultation with their fellow members. Not all such promises of support could be met immediately but in the longer term they can contribute to the advance of the cause or interest in question. A deflationary cycle in the integrative system is marked by a tendency to question the reputation of those who wield influence and by an increasing

24

insistence on narrow in-groupism in its exercise. Conversely, inflationary cycles are marked by broken promises of support and unjustified claims to wield influence.[34]

Lastly, in the cultural subsystem charismatic leaders can employ their moral authority to expand commitments. Parsons argues that charismatic innovation does not involve a total break with the established value system but represents an extension of the values. This will not be inflationary provided it is the first stage in institutionalisation. Inflationary pressures stem from a failure to develop effective implementative procedures corresponding to the growth of commitments: that is, the charismatic movement must be routinised. Deflation would ensue where such stringent conditions were imposed on the implementation of new values that either charismatic innovation is impossible or its initial stages were so opposed by moral absolutists that the charismatic movement was forced to withdraw. Charismatic innovations vary in their articulation with previously established institutional patterns. There are four main possibilities: (a) extinction of the movement owing to its insufficient articulation; (b) a smooth institutionalisation owing to innovation occurring in relatively minor subsystems; (c) a schismatic revolutionary movement along the lines of social and cultural cleavages; or (d) generalisation of the values to include both innovative and established systems within a higher-order system. The greater the value generalisation the greater the possibility of a fundamentalist revolt against current patterns and levels of implementation; the less the value generalisation the greater the possibility of extinction or schism. Thus in differentiated cultural systems there is an inherent possibility of cultural breakdown or conflict.[35]

We have now completed our review of normative functionalist approaches to the analysis of social order and social change. We have neglected the primarily analytical and static aspects of the approach (e.g. the pattern variables, the location of different concrete structures within the total social system, the intricacies of the interactive process, the internal organisation of the components of action) and the application of the framework to various empirical problems.[36] But the significance of value consensus, the functional problems and structural differentiation should now be obvious. Likewise the more important lacunae in the normative functionalist approach should also be apparent. Thus the role of non-normative factors is nowhere treated in detail comparable to that accorded normative elements; there

25

is little concern with the factors that determine the variability of values and their relative historical importance; there is little discussion of how strains develop within the system prior to their manifestation in social and psychological disturbances; there is little recognition of the often non-solidary character of subsocietal and especially societal systems; and so forth. But some of the wilder charges against normative functionalism can also be recognised as inaccurate and ill-founded. Normative functionalism *is* concerned with power, with force, with change, with revolution, etc.; it is the way in which it deals with these that is open to criticism. A marked contrast is to be found in the analyses of constraint and conflict theorists – who are concerned with those factors and processes that are most often neglected by normative functionalists in their search for universal categories applicable to the analysis of social and non-social subsystems of action alike. It is to a consideration of such theories that we now turn.

Constraint Theories

Whereas a common value system serves as the major point of reference for normative functionalists, conflict theorists stress the notion of a social system based on the constraint of some by others. The nature of such constraint varies, however, with the particular branch of conflict theory advocated. Classical Marxist theory sees constraint as grounded primarily in the relations of production and modified by a superstructure of legal, political, religious and other social relations. Later theories see these constraints grounded primarily in the distribution of authority[37] or even in control over the content of shared values in an hegemonic order.[38] In each case, however, social order in the sense of peaceful coexistence in the operation of social institutions is related to a normative order. This is seen most obviously in the concept of hegemony or ruling ideology but it is also present in the notion of authority as legitimate power.[39] The really crucial difference between constraint and consensus theories is not therefore to be found in a differential focus on values and interests but in their approach to the analysis of value systems. This distinction is underlined by a consideration of the major axes of cultural variation in the two theories. Normative functionalists see the major axis as running from institutionalisation through to anomie.[40] Constraint theorists see the major axis as running from institutionalisation of the ruling ideology through trade-union or

26

bloc consciousness to genuine class-conscious opposition.[41] Thus the essential difference between conflict and consensus theorists is the notion of constraint (internal and external) and its implication for value analysis.[42]

Classical Marxist theory rests ultimately on the ambiguous distinction between the economic base and the superstructure of society.[43] The economic base consists in the mode of production dominant in society. The superstructure comprises the remaining legal, political, social, religious and other institutional and ideological forms in the society.[44] The mode of production is defined not only by the technical forces of production but also by the division of labour and the relations of production.[45] In the bourgeois society, for example, the relations of production consist essentially in the institution of capitalist private property and the class relations defined by the distribution of such property. It is important to realise that property develops differently in different historical epochs – there are important variations in the social formations of tribal, ancient slave-owning, feudal serf-owning, capitalist, communist, and Oriental societies. A definition of bourgeois property thus involves a complete description of the social conditions of capitalist production. And the rise of the joint-stock company and of co-operative production are several times held to effect a fundamental alteration in class relations.[46] Variation in the forces of production and in the nature and distribution of property are thus key factors in the explanation of social structure and the dynamics of social change.

The nature and distribution of property define class relations. They do so through their influence on the economic condition of different classes, on the distribution of political power, and on the dominant values and beliefs of the society. Property ownership provides the basis for the exercise of social as well as purely economic power and finds its practical and ideal expression in a particular form of the State and of political relations that corresponds to the particular type of ownership.[47] Likewise the nature and distribution of property affects the historical importance of ideas and encourages the dominance of the values and views espoused by property owners and their intellectual apologists.[48] There is thus a complex chain of relations between technology, economic relations, political power and ideological and cultural relations. The emergence of economically conditioned political, social and cultural phenomena is followed by their partial autonomy and feedback on to the economic base.[49]

27

Not only do the nature and distribution of property define class relations, they also necessarily define a system of opposing class interests – interests which precede the emergence of class consciousness and which are inherently antagonistic.[50] In every epoch there are essentially two classes whose interests are directly opposed and contradictory – slave-owner and slave, landlord and serf, capitalist and wage-earner. But in any concrete historical situation there will a greater variety of classes and political conflict groups due to the survival of some sectors from previous epochs, to the differential development of the technical forces of production, to the imperfect realisation of true class consciousness, to the impact of variations in market situation, and so on. These differences are overridden as the main conflict assumes a greater historical importance under the impact of increasing proletarianisation of intermediate classes and increasing immiseration of the oppressed.[51] The force that creates class consciousness is the increasing contradiction between the forces and the relations of production.[52] Initially the relations of production facilitate the development of these technological forces : the bourgeoisie in the early stages of capitalism thus constitutes a progressive force. But the realisation of the full potential of these new forces of production comes into conflict with the interests of the bourgeoisie in maintaining the existing pattern of relations which enables the exploitation of the proletariat through the appropriation of their surplus labour. This conflict becomes apparent through the increasing pauperisation of the proletariat, the falling rate of profit and the increasingly acute commercial crises due to the overproduction of commodities.[53] Thus the proletariat comes into conflict with the bourgeoisie and, during the ensuing struggle, develops an awareness of its position as a class-for-itself in economic and political competition with the capitalist class.[54] The outcome of their struggle, other things being equal, is the overthrow of the property-owning class and the establishment of a dictatorship of the proletariat as a prelude to the introduction of a truly communist state. This revolution can be achieved either through the ballot-box or, which is more likely, through a violent confrontation with the State and the repressive apparatus.[55]

The classical Marxist model allows for all six stages of the value-added process outlined by Smelser in the genesis of collective behaviour. It is quite clear that the proletarian revolution can occur only in a specific historical epoch and at a particular

28

period within that epoch itself. The structured strain is shown to be a systemic contradiction that results in inadequate functioning : its primary manifestation being the emergent contradiction between the forces and relations of production. The generalised beliefs are those of theoretical class consciousness and it is explicitly recognised that these can predate the political organisation of the working class and that in such circumstances it comprises merely utopian thought.[56] The precipitants are to be found in the crises of capitalism – crises which are bound to become more and more acute owing to the objective dynamics of the capitalist system. The exercise of social control and the mobilisation of the participants for action are found, respectively, in the repressive operations of the state apparatus in its role of the executive arm of the bourgeoisie and in the development of trade union and labour party organisation. Demonstration of this correspondence is by no means intended to emphasise the superiority or inferiority of either normative functionalism or conflict theories in their approach to social movements. Rather it is intended to demonstrate the possibilities of assimilation and synthesis.

It is well known that Marx's predictions about the future development of capitalist society were not wholly accurate. However, this does not mean that his theoretical model is totally invalidated or that his empirical work is completely erroneous. It does mean, on the other hand, that the conceptual scheme is in need of revision. And it is to the theoretical contributions of three such revisionists[57] that we now turn.

Whereas the classical Marxist emphasis is on the economic foundations of society and thus the economic origins of conflict, Dahrendorf sees authority relations as the dominant factor in the determination of class relations and the genesis of class conflict. The central thesis of his revision is that ownership of the means of production is simply a special – and outdated – case of the exercise of authority. A general theory of class conflict must redefine the nature of class in terms of superordination and subordination in imperatively co-ordinated associations. Having thus redefined the nature of class, Dahrendorf proceeds to elaborate a symbolic model of class conflict.

He argues that in every imperatively co-ordinated group those with, and those without, authority constitute two quasi-groups or latent groups with opposite, antithetic interests. Such quasi-groups become manifest interest groups which engage in more or

29

less intense and more or less violent conflict to the extent that certain conditions are present. These conditions include freedom of association, freedom of communication, availability of organisers, availability of ideologists and a socially structured pattern of recruitment. Given these conditions the class conflict that follows will vary both in intensity and in violence. The intensity of conflict varies positively with the degree of superimposition of cleavages and the crystallisation of class boundaries. The violence of class conflict varies inversely with the relativity of deprivations felt by the subordinate class, the effectiveness of institutionalised conflict regulation mechanisms, and the legitimacy accorded to the conflict by the authorities. Finally the extent of social change that results is determined by the intensity of conflict; and the suddenness of change is positively related to the violence of conflict. Such, in broad outline, is Dahrendorf's general theory of conflict and change.[58]

More recently Dahrendorf has argued that 'neither the classical nor the revised theory of class conflict can cope with the political condition of the modern world'.[59] The classical Marxist theory failed to account adequately for changes in class structure, the institutionalisation of class conflict, the occurrence of revolutions in the less developed capitalist societies, and so forth. The revised theory failed to account for such phenomena as the absence of socialism in the United States, the emergence of fascism in inter-war Europe, the lack of opposition in the Soviet Union and the secularisation of politics in the post-war period.[60] Accordingly Dahrendorf suggests the relaxation of a further postulate of conflict theory—that the only adequate, or even the only possible, expression for social relations of constraint is group-conflict.[61] Whereas his class theory focused on the conditions which facilitated or inhibited the *possibility* of realising interests collectively, the revised theory emphasises those conditions which obviate the *need* to realise interests collectively. In particular the individual need not mobilise in solidary collective formations when it is possible to advance his interests alone or in more limited pluralistic interest groups. The existence of high levels of social mobility over time is especially important in facilitating such individuation of class conflict.

This alleged revision does not really modify the theory of class conflict. The conditions that obviate the necessity for a collective mobilisation are all mentioned in the original formulation as conditions that intervene in the formation of class conflict groups.

The role of social mobility was emphasised in the crystallisation of class boundaries and in the patterning of the recruitment base.[62] The plurality of interest groups is a simple reflection of the non-superimposition of conflicts. Dahrendorf has therefore merely shifted the empirical focus of his investigations rather than revised the original theoretical framework.[63] The revision thus contains the same two major problems as the first formulation. We must question the priority of authority relations in the determination of conflict – especially as conflict is more likely when authority relations are superimposed on other (non-authoritative) lines of cleavage.[64] And secondly there is a systematic neglect of the role of shared beliefs in the genesis of class conflict – a role that is stressed by normative functionalist and classical Marxist alike and that is indispensable in the mobilisation of interest groups for the attainment of public goods.[65] In his concern with the institutionalisation of conflict and with the reaction of authority, however, Dahrendorf has made a significant contribution to the development of conflict theory.

In the light of Dahrendorf's revision it is important to revisit Marxist theories of the state. In this connection the work of Lenin and Gramsci is particularly interesting but we first examine the views of Marx and Engels.

For both Marx and Engels the state is an epiphenomenon of the class struggle. It originates in the need to regulate this struggle and it represents the interests of the economically dominant class in this regulation. When, where, and to what extent the state arises, depends directly on when, where and to what extent the class antagonisms of a given society are incapable of objective reconciliation.[66] Occasionally the class struggle is so evenly balanced that the state can acquire some degree of independence by the manipulation of class divisions. Thus the absolute monarchies of seventeenth- and eighteenth-century Europe played off the nobility against the bourgeoisie and Bonapartism played off the bourgeoisie against the proletariat.[67] Even in less exceptional periods the state may be run by only a fraction of the ruling class or by an economically subordinate class that none the less represents the interests of the ruling class.[68] Either of these two possibilities may make the state less rigid but will not fundamentally influence the class character of the state. In addition to its class character there are three other major features of the state : its territorial basis of organisation, the existence of armed forces independent of the citizenry as a whole, and the imposition of taxes to finance the state apparatus and its activities.[69] The Asiatic state stands outside this basic schema because it exists to provide the means of production (i.e. irrigation and other water-works) rather than to represent the interests of a ruling class independent of and prior to the state. The Asiatic state is not an epiphenomenon but the dominant force in Oriental society. It confronts the mass of the population as landlord and sovereign and its administration can be seen as the authentic rulers of the society.[70] Later Marxist writers have argued that this Asiatic state is in fact the state form corresponding to feudal property and ownership but this is clearly not the intention behind the original formulation.[71]

Lenin stands right within the main Marxist tradition in this respect and emphasises the class character of the state. He argues that the capitalist state must be overthrown by a violent prole-tarian revolution and that only after the revolution and the socialisation of the means of production can the proletarian state wither away.[72] He follows Marx in arguing that whereas all previous revolutions improved the state bureaucracy and armed forces, the proletarian revolution will destroy both these instru-ments of repression. Lenin includes England and America in this analysis on the grounds that both have developed bureaucratic and military machines since Marx wrote of the possibility of peaceful revolution.[73] The overthrow of the state will occur only through the mobilisation of the proletariat by a vanguard party which raises the level of working-class consciousness from an economistic trade-union consciousness to a full political aware-ness of the need to destroy the capitalist order and the capitalist state. Without such a vanguard the working class will remain subordinate to the bourgeoisie and the bourgeois state; for it is capable of developing only a trade-union level of awareness in its absence.[74]

Gramsci develops these views further. He rejects the economic determinism inherent in much Marxist theory[75] and reformulates the nature of the state in Western societies to give it more autonomy and a less repressive role. Gramsci seems to have accepted the repressive view of the state in the analysis of Asiatic and semi-Asiatic societies. But he asserts the distinctiveness of Western bourgeois society and its state system. In the West the function of *dominio* (repression) is complemented by that of *egemonia* (mobilisation of consent). Indeed the superstructure of advanced capitalist societies has developed so much autonomy

32

that it is an effective social and historical force that reacts back on the infrastructure. It is only in periods of acute crisis that resort to force is necessary or normal. At other times consent is mobilised by intellectuals and civil institutions such as the Church, the schools, unions, mass media, political parties and family. There are also intellectuals who represent the interest of the oppressed classes, however, and who develop their level of awareness through the elaboration of a coherent hegemonic ideological alternative. The quality and duration of the revolutionary movement is then dependent on the quality and coherence of the hegemony developed by intellectuals and proletariat prior to seizure of power. The strategy appropriate to such societies is a gradualist strategy involving participation in bourgeois institutions together with the simultaneous subversion and replacement of the bourgeois hegemony. In Asiatic and other repressive systems, on the other hand, the appropriate strategy remains that of violent overthrow of the state apparatus.[76]

The solution offered by constraint theory to the problem of order is thus similar in several respects to that of normative functionalism in its emphasis on the role of normative order. In Gramsci's work, however, it is held to be the normal mode of regulating social life and is the key factor in historical materialism. The significance of normative order is underlined if we remember that the economic base comprises not only the forces of production but also the division of labour and property institutions and that the latter factors have a normative dimension and cannot be discussed without reference to normative specification of rights and obligations. The superstructure is essentially a residual phenomenon and is not to be identified with the totality of norms and values in society. The essential difference between the two perspectives lies in the functions assigned to the normative order. Normative functionalists do not really subscribe to the 'interest' interpretation of cultural systems and tend to ignore the determination of dominant values and the development of contra-cultural systems. Constraint theorists see the superstructure of ideas, beliefs, and symbols as an expression of the interests of the dominant class and an instrument, more or less intentional, of the subordination of oppressed classes. In addition, of course, constraint theorists are much more likely to emphasise the role of coercion and repression in the maintenance of social order. These differences are open to empirical investigation, however, and can thus be treated as variables in a general theory without undue distortion of either constraint or normative functionalist theories.

Exchange Theories

Normative functionalism stresses common values and the normative regulation of social interaction. Constraint theories emphasise the universality of external constraint and the differentiation of power in social systems. Exchange theories examine the existential aspects of interaction between equals and between unequals and the emergence of power relations and normative orders. Although constraint theorists certainly employ the notion of exploitation and Parsons considers the interchange of factor inputs and outputs, it is exchange theories that pay particular attention to variations in the conditions, the rates and the effects of exchange. However, exchange theories have tended deliberately to focus on the sub-institutional levels of interaction – the actions of individuals prior to the stabilisation of interaction and/or their actions within the constraints set by normative rules and obligations.[77] It is at the macrosocietal level that exchange theory is least articulated and yet most useful; we must therefore consider the relevance of exchange theory to macrosocial analysis rather than its important contributions to the study of microsocial interaction.[78]

Blau has defined social exchange as 'any behaviour oriented to socially mediated goals'.[79] The problem of order is thus also central to exchange theory – indeed it is difficult to distinguish between exchange defined in this way and the total field of social interaction. However, Blau also provides a typology of exchange relations based on a cross classification of modes and objects of social exchange. The mode of exchange can be either reciprocal or unilateral; the object of exchange can be either intrinsic or extrinsic. Thus there are four basic types of microsocial interaction : mutual attraction and one-sided attachments in the exchange of intrinsic rewards; and 'exchange relations' and power relations in the extrinsic sphere.[80] At the macrosocial level mutual attraction is held to have its functional equivalent in the sharing of basic values which creates integrative bonds of solidarity.[81] Likewise exchange relations find their equivalent in the economic institutions of society and political organisation corresponds to power relations.[82] Although there is no mention of a macrosocial equivalent to unilateral attachments the deference

34

system of the wider society would seem to be just such a pheno-menon.[83] Exchange theory thus recognises the significance of values at the macrosocial level and indeed seems to rely on them as a *deus ex machina* for the maintenance of social order at the macrolevel of organisation.

At the microlevel shared values are initially less important. It is the expectation of rewards (intrinsic and/or extrinsic) that makes association among actors attractive. Likewise it is this expectation that makes actors in emergent groups compete for esteem that is based on their ability to make contributions to the group. Those that can indeed make essential contributions attain superior status and, where the benefits they provide cannot readily be obtained elsewhere and cannot be reciprocated in kind, they also acquire power over those who derive advantage from the continued existence of the association. The powerful can continue to exercise power to the extent that they are able to supply these advantages; to close off alternative sources of supply; to back up their power with coercive force; and to in-crease the dependence of those less powerful through ideological means.[84] If such power is exercised 'fairly' in accordance with given standards of justice it is legitimated.[85] Otherwise opposition will emerge on the basis of joint exploitation and commitments to the exploited group.[86] This emergence of opposition is particularly likely where power is based, not on the unilateral provision of goods and services, but on command over means of coercion.

It is not altogether clear whence the standards of justice derive. Gouldner talks of a norm of reciprocity as universal and antece-dent to interaction whereas Blau considers this norm to be an emergent cultural property that regulates and limits exchange relations.[87] In addition, whatever the sources of the norm of reciprocity, there is the problem of what defines the equivalence of benefits – does equivalence rest on cultural definition or on psychological satisfaction, does equivalence depend on costs as well as benefits and so forth?[88] Implicit in macrosocial exchange theory is an alternative solution to these problems. Blau notes that cultural traditions contain a 'counterinstitutional component' that consists of those basic values and ideals that have not been expressed in explicit institutional forms. The conflict between these as yet unrealised, but culturally legitimated, ideals and the actual conditions of social existence can provide a basis for social opposition to existing institutions.[89] The existence of such counter-institutional values and their development into an ideology of

35

opposition would seem to provide one alternative solution to the genesis of opposition and one that is not dependent on a norm of reciprocity.

Consideration of reciprocities led Blau to formulate the important idea that reciprocities in one respect generate imbalances in other respects, and vice versa. Thus the unilateral provision of services can be balanced by inequalities of power. And the exploitative use of power can be balanced by the emergence of opposition. Power imbalances are particularly relevant because of their *potentially* disruptive effects on social order: the actual extent of disruption depends on the advantages to be derived from submission since these may outweigh the costs involved in the experience of domination.[90] Thus exchange theory lays particular emphasis on the relative costs and benefits to be gained from social relationships rather than on the simple facts of subordination or superordination.

A further emphasis is on the emergent properties of macro-social structure.[91] Whereas the structure of small groups evolves as their members interact, there is no direct interaction among most members of the larger society. Some other mechanisms must exist, therefore, to mediate their interactions: according to Blau these mechanisms include not only interdependence between sub-structures, and exchange and power relations between organised groups, but also social norms and shared values. The latter provide the matrix within which individuals and groups interact and ensure social order through the legitimation of authority and the acceptance of moral standards that prohibit flagrant exploitation. Conformity with such standards provides individuals with social approval from those not directly involved in an exchange and with peace of mind and so rewards them for their contribution to the maintenance of social order. Shared values facilitate the extension of interaction beyond the limits of particular face-to-face groups both in time and space. Thus legitimating values extend the scope of political organisation through freeing it from dependence not only on the direct exercise of power but also on particular incumbents and offices. Likewise opposition ideals serve to extend the scope of opposition beyond the limits of the influence of individual agitators to all whose existential conditions predispose them towards these ideals. Similarly universalistic values provide generalised criteria of evaluation in social exchange and thus contribute to the emergence of social strata based on rewards for the differential provision of valued goods

36

and services. Lastly particularistic values serve to delimit the boundaries and identities of subgroups and collectivities larger than face-to-face groups. Without such shared values social organisation and reorganisation on a societal level would be impossible.[92]

The complex patterns of social interaction mediated by common values become institutionalised and are thus perpetuated from generation to generation. Successful institutionalisation depends on three conditions. Firstly, the organisational principles and procedures must be formalised and embodied in offices and structures rather than specific persons. Secondly, the social values that legitimate these institutions must be transmitted in the socialisation process. And, thirdly, the dominant groups in the community must be strongly identified with these values and support them.[93] Once institutionalised, these values and organisations will constitute external constraints for individual members of the society and so factors to which they must adapt. Also implicit in the cultural tradition, however, will be the counter-institutional principles that provide a latent source of justification for dissent when the disjunction between ideal and social reality is too great. In this way individuals are able to overcome the structural constraints imposed by the historical development of social organisation.

The exchange theory propounded by Blau remains more or less firmly within the sociological tradition. Other types of exchange theory rely more heavily on economic concepts and models. Whereas sociologically oriented exchange theories are not concerned primarily with the derivation of empirical hypotheses from explicitly stated assumptions, economically oriented exchange theories are so concerned. For example, Curry and Wade have analysed the genesis of the French Revolution in terms of exchange theories relating to administrative recruitment markets. An examination of their argument will illustrate this point.

In the administrative recruitment market there is an exchange of administrative skills and power in policy-making. There are three important demand schedules for the determination of the equilibrium points : (a) the demand schedule showing the quantity of élite appointments demanded at each cost level of acquiring the skills useful in administration; (b) the supply schedule showing the quantity of administrative appointments offered at each level of skill useful in administration; and (c) a reservation demand schedule that shows the absolute level of administrative appointments the élite is prepared or capable of offering – regardless of the level of skill required by the group and regardless of whether this quantity is more or less than the equilibrium quantity of appointments. The equilibrium point is of course defined by the intersection of the demand and supply schedules. Where the reservation demand is less than this equilibrium point there is necessarily a conflict generated by the impossibility of an efficient market solution. Instability in the market can be eliminated by governmental intervention or a revolutionary incursion to shift the reservation demand schedule and produce an equilibrium. Such intervention may also affect the other two schedules, however, and thereby create a fresh disequilibrium. Other changes may also affect the demand and supply schedules for administrative appointments. Such changes include variations in the costs of training, shifts in alternative employment opportunities, increases in the demand for governmental outputs, and so forth. The French Revolution of 1789 is explained in part by the failure of the government to alter the reserve demand schedule to a new equilibrium point at a time when the administrative and legal middle classes were denied access to government appointments by the intransigence and even retrenchment of the nobility in their control over such positions. Thus the alteration of political recruitment conditions in favour of the middle class and, less convincingly, the decentralisation of administration were the almost inevitable results of the revolution.[94]

Mitchell has recently labelled this sort of exchange theory 'political economy'.[95] He argues that it is concerned primarily with the interchanges between government and citizens in markets for private and public goods, services and resources, for controls over behaviour and demands for such control, and for political support and opportunities for income, status and the like. There are a number of differences between the market economy and the public economy which ensure that the co-ordination of the political market is not automatic and decentralised as in a competitive market economy. Thus decisions about the allocation of resources are not necessarily determined by the ability to pay and so there must be centralised mechanisms of control over the allocation of resources and the imposition of burdens. Political economies must also develop ways and means of adapting and stabilising the environment. All of these problems, it is argued, can be considered in a logical, deductive, mathematical way and require the development of formalised models of decision-making in various degrees of certainty and uncertainty.[96]

One of the interesting problems raised by this more formal exchange theory is why individuals participate in social movements at all. In any large, latent group each individual member will find it to his advantage if all the costs or sacrifices necessary to achieve the collective goals or interests of the group are incurred by others. For any benefits that are realised for the group will come whether or not any given individual participates in their realisation; thus it is in the interests of every member to concentrate on his private affairs and allow others to work for the collective good. Thus there is an obstacle to the organisation of any large group that can be overcome only by the use of sanctions and selective incentives for participation. These sanctions range from shared commitments and informal pressures in smaller groups through the provision of benefits which can be enjoyed only by participants or contributors to the use of coercion and terrorism against those who do not participate. Wherever we find an organisation or social movement that aims to provide such collective goods, therefore, we must look for the sanctions that underly support for the movement.[97] In the absence of such sanctions even groups that are flagrantly exploited may not organise against their oppressors.

Thus we see that exchange theories also have much to contribute to the analysis of social order, reform and revolution. The distinctive contributions of exchange theory is in its focus upon the existential conditions of interaction within the limits given by normative and structural constraints. It deals more fully with this aspect of social order than either normative functionalism or constraint theories and thus provides a necessary complement to their concern with values and power relations. In addition its concern with both the costs and benefits of social action underlines the dangers of overemphasis on either the antagonistic or the non-antagonistic nature of social relations.

Conclusions

In this comparatively lengthy chapter we have been concerned with the presentation in broad outline of three main perspectives on social order and social change. Our concern with exposition has been detrimental to effective criticism and the elaboration of finer points and qualifying statements in the various writers. In our next chapter we shall examine the major points of comparison and contrast between the three perspectives; and in Chapter 4 we shall present the outlines of an analytical framework for the investigation of social order and change. Both these chapters provide an opportunity for an elaboration and criticism of certain crucial features of the different theories. To these tasks we now turn.

3 Some Emergent Themes in the Study of Order

A major argument in this study is that there exists a theoretical convergence in structural analysis and thus a possibility of a synthesis of contemporary perspectives to provide a new and coherent analytical framework. Earlier work in this area has tended to compare and contrast only the 'consensus' and 'conflict' models and has reached one or more of three conclusions. Firstly, that the two theories display many parallels; secondly, that they have a differential utility according to the area of application; and, thirdly, that integration is possible at the cost of sacrificing the distinctive focus of each model.[1] Most studies have merely pointed to the obvious parallels and differential utility of the two models and no substantial theoretical synthesis over the whole range of structural analysis has been attempted.[2] This is particularly unfortunate as the loss of a distinctive focus is *not* a necessary feature of theoretical synthesis. It is likely only where common themes or concepts *or* an exclusive set of assumptions are employed. To the extent that due attention is paid not only to the common themes but also to the exclusive elements in the different conceptual schemes and that the articulating assumptions are integrated, if necessary through the development of hypotheses explaining their variability in concrete situations, then a genuine synthesis of a high order may be possible. The possibilities of such a synthesis have been underlined by recent developments in macrosocial exchange theory which would seem to provide a real point of convergence between the conflict and consensus models and also to suggest that each is concerned with different aspects of the same phenomenon rather than with entirely different phenomena. It is for this reason that we examined the three competing models in the previous chapter and that we now turn to an examination of joint concerns and emergent themes in this chapter.

It should be clear that the three theoretical frameworks in the preceding chapter are indeed complementary in many respects. They are concerned with the general analysis of social structure and process and with the interrelations between social order and

41

social change.[3] Within this overall framework they certainly exhibit considerable specialisation and consequently each leaves uninvestigated or unconceptualised certain *crucial* areas of social analysis. Reference to these problematic areas is confined to *ad hoc* invocations and to residual categories.[4] What is particularly interesting, therefore, is that these three theories have tended to elaborate each other's residual categories and thus contribute to the possibility of a higher level synthesis which allows full play to all the crucial factors in structural analysis. The elimination of residual categories in favour of positively defined analytical categories is an important aspect of the development of scientific knowledge and the successful synthesis of these different analytical frameworks should contribute to the advance of sociological theory. The following chapters represent just one attempt at such a combination.

Our basic strategy is to turn the residual categories of the different theories into positively defined categories and articulate them with the more general scheme that results. This can be achieved in part by the application of the different theories to each other to provide the basic analytical framework and through the recombination of their assumptions to provide the necessary means of deriving hypotheses. Thus normative functionalist concepts can be applied, for example, to the internal structure and external relations of the economy (material substratum) and thus reveal the significance of values and norms in its operation as well as the important interchanges between the economy and the rest of society (superstructure). Likewise constraint theories can be applied to the analysis of all four functional subsystems and so reveal the significance of inequalities in access to control over the functioning of society and the determinants of the historical importance of different value systems. And exchange theories can be applied to the interaction of norm and substratum to demonstrate the independent role of exchange in the determination of social structure and dynamics – the area most neglected by both normative functionalists and constraint theorists.[5] The actual extent of consensus, constraint, equality, inequality, reciprocity and exploitation will be treated as variables and an attempt will be made to generate their causes and effects on the basis of the analytical framework and its assumptions. We now turn to a consideration of the more or less joint concerns of the different structural theories and to the more important emergent themes.

The Problem of Order

The most obvious joint concern is the problem of order. The problem is certainly formulated in different terms in each of the models but it is resolved in a similar way. All three stress the role of normative order in securing social order. For the consensus theorists this is axiomatic; for the conflict theorists it is problematic but seemingly inevitable outside of revolutionary situations; and for the exchange theorists it is simply emergent and contingent on exchange relations. The constraint theorists also emphasise the role of non-normative factors in the determination of social order and they are more likely to stress the ideological functions of value systems. Any synthesis must therefore be concerned with the analysis of value systems and their articulation with social structure. To achieve such a synthesis it will be necessary to translate certain apparent axioms of the two main theories into variables and then develop hypotheses to explain the nature and causes of their variation. The *de facto* normative functionalist axiom of consensus must become a variable and so must the constraint theorists' apparent assumption that value systems are always ideological representations of the interests of the dominant (economic) class. The exchange theorists have tended to make both assumptions dependent variables within their basic scheme and thus avoid the problems associated with such rigorous assumptions.

Justification for this procedure can readily be found in the theoretical analyses of both normative functionalists and conflict theorists. Thus Parsons' treatment of the American value system and his discussion of stratification both display an emphasis on the central value system; while his analyses of McCarthyism, the charismatic innovation, and social change generally, give recognition to the role of power and dissensus.[6] Similarly Smelser's analysis of collective behaviour and the more general dynamics of social change also show an interest in the breakdown of consensus and the role of the government-and-control apparatus in restoring social order. Lastly Parsons seems to recognise that values and stratification are maintained primarily by a dominant class in arguing that differentiation and adaptive upgrading make it increasingly difficult to maintain a class system in which one class is excluded from full membership in the societal community by another, superior class.[7] Blau likewise pays attention

43

to the importance of both dominant social groups in the maintenance of institutions and of values in the maintenance of power. Conversely constraint theorists are prepared to concede that values have an inherent dynamic of their own, independent of their relations to the infrastructure, and that they play an important role in the organisation of the economy.[8] Thus each of the theories treats, albeit intermittently, both consensus and 'ideology' as variables.

Cultural analysis is thus essential to any synthesis of these models – not only because of its significance in consensus theory but also because of its central role in each theory. In any case the meaning of behaviour would have to be considered in any sociological analysis of action – action is after all subjectively meaningful behaviour and these meanings, both cultural and psychological, cannot be ignored. Their organisation and creation are thus important aspects of any sociological theory and so necessarily of the present theory. Furthermore, the emergent properties of culture have an independent influence on social interaction and social order and these influences must also be included within the analytical framework.

In our synthesis, therefore, we shall draw on all three models to illuminate the analysis of culture. From normative functionalism we take the important idea that culture is one of four systems of action and that it serves to maintain the basic (i.e. central) patterns of interaction in the social system. Thus we distinguish between American and Soviet societies in terms of their values and normative order (including relations of production) rather than in terms of their forces of production (which are industrial in both cases). From constraint theories we take the equally important notion that values can serve interests and that they can generate oppositional movements. It is thus necessary to examine the role of structure in determining the historical importance and functions of culture and also the distribution of control over the creation and interpretation, specification and implementation of values. Finally from exchange theory we take the notion of emergence and consider how cultural change is linked to structural dynamics.

The Problem of Power

A second common theme is the analysis of sanctions and power relations. The problem of order is essentially a problem of power and its regulation. Interaction involves a *double contingency* in which each individual or group action represents a sanction – reward or punishment – for the actions of others and vice versa.[9] It is the conflict inherent in this situation that creates our basic problem. None of the three theories denies the importance of power and coercion in social interaction. The generation of power and the control of coercion is a functional imperative in normative functionalism; the universality of external constraint or domination is axiomatic in conflict theory;[10] and the emergence of unilateral dependence and the significance of coercion are emphasised by exchange theory. Furthermore, Parsons explicitly recognises the role of non-normative sanctions and, at least in his recent writings, argues that the zero-sum character of power is just as important as its collective character. Thus he writes of power deflation involving the resort to force in which the interests of a minority are preserved at the expense of the majority.[11] Similarly Blau stresses two aspects of power relations – internal and external. Whereas within the collectivity power tends to be legitimate and its exercise beneficial to the less powerful, in the relations between collectivities power tends to be exploitative and detrimental to the interests of the less powerful.[12] This duality seems to combine the contributions of both consensus and conflict theory. For the former treats societies as a form of solidary collectivity, while the latter treats them as congeries of at least latent collectivities with conflicting interests based on differential power.[13] Thus Parsons can assume that the goals of an élite are collective goals shared by the whole society; and the conflict theorists can assume that they are antithetic to the interests of the non-élite. Where class conflict has been eliminated through the introduction of communal ownership, however, even classical Marxist theorists see leadership as genuinely collective and beneficial to the led.[14] It seems justified, therefore, to treat both the solidarity of societies and the exploitativeness of power as variables and to attempt an explanation of their variation.

In the synthesis we therefore treat the relative solidarity of societies as a variable in the same way that we treat consensus; and we allow for variation in the exploitativeness of power just as in the ideological functions of values. We also extend the analysis of power by inclusion of the four types of sanctions elaborated by Parsons – allowing not only for economic and politico-military power but also for influence and commitments.[15] From exchange theory we take the idea that power can be emergent as well as imposed and we examine the conditions of its emergence. Likewise the zero-sum and non-zero-sum aspects of power will receive considerable attention and different types of power model will be examined.

Exchange Relations

A third common theme is that of exchange. This is of course the primary focus of exchange theory but it also receives significant attention from both normative functionalist and constraint theorists. The normative functionalists pay particular attention to the sociology of markets not only in the economy but also in the interchange between functional subsystems – although these can be located empirically only when there is structural differentiation of a high degree between the subsystems – and between leaders and followers in a variety of contexts. Similarly classical Marxists are concerned with exploitation – which is only a special type of exchange relation – and neo-Marxist theories examine the rate of exploitation as a variable. The theory of surplus value is an exchange concept *par excellence* and plays an important part in classical Marxism.[16] The characteristic focus of constraint theory would seem to be on exchanges between collectivities with differential power rather than actors (individual or collective) with differential functions – although the classical analysis of the three classes based on land, labour and capital could be argued to enter this latter category. Normative functionalists, on the other hand, are more concerned with the interdependence and interchanges between functionally differentiated units and are less likely to consider power a constant owing to the inherent strains towards both inflationary and deflationary cycles. Exchange theories of course consider both types of social exchange.

In the ensuing synthesis we shall employ the insights of such exchange theory to the dynamics of exchange between different power groups and between different functional groups. We shall also be concerned with the extent to which functional and power differentials coincide or differ. The rate of exploitation, reciprocity or benefaction will also receive consideration and must be treated as a variable. Finally we shall be particularly interested in inflationary and deflationary cycles.

Structural Differentiation

A fourth theme common to all three theories is that of structural differentiation. The normative functionalist approach to this phenomenon is particularly well known; but we find an examination of the process within both exchange and constraint theories. Marx and Engels were particularly interested in what they called the division of labour and the ways in which newly differentiated social groups acquired a measure of autonomy from the material substratum.[17] Moreover, Marx gave a detailed account of the manner in which labour was differentiated from familial relations and of the impact of large-scale industry on the traditional family – concerns which Smelser shared in his analysis of social change and the industrial revolution.[18] Likewise Marx investigated the differentiation of religion and the state and used as an index of this process the degree of political emancipation of the Jews.[19] There are also striking parallels between Parsons' account of money and Marx's discussion of the emergence of money as the result of structural differentiation. The latter also noted how the emergence of money permits not only the monetary mediation of commodity exchange but also the mediation by commodities of monetary accumulation. There are obvious parallels to this phenomenon in other functional subsystems – in military conquest, in electioneering, in status mobility, and so forth. Later conflict theorists have shown less interest in structural differentiation but analyses such as Dahrendorf's that stress the role of super-imposition and cross-cutting cleavages certainly depend on this concept. Exchange theory is of course closely concerned with the idea of differentiation – especially as this is manifested in the division of labour and the concomitant pattern of 'organic solidarity' based on interdependence.

The present synthesis will therefore also include the notion of structural differentiation in its conceptual framework. We intend to follow the analysis laid down by the normative functionalists since it is the most systematic and elaborate but we also emphasise the variable nature of its effects and the possibilities it creates for increased exploitation as well as increased co-operation. We also accept the implications of structural differentiation for the emergence of media of exchange and other means of securing compliance in a differentiated system. And we shall naturally emphasise the important problems of order and stability that are created by differentiation.

Social Movements

Of the three general perspectives under review it is social

47

exchange theory that is least original and articulate about social movements. The contribution of more economistic exchange theories to the organisation of social movements deserves attention, however, and it will be incorporated into the synthesis. The sociologically oriented exchange theorist's model is basically that exploitation engenders opposition rather than acquiescence only when the incidence of exploitation is socially structured and when communication among the exploited is possible. Conflict theory is more incisive on this matter – not only on class movements but also for such phenomena as cargo cults, millennial movements, social banditry, liberation movements, and so forth.[20] Generally, however, it is Smelser's analysis of collective behaviour that provides the most useful initial framework but it will need considerable refinement to match the demands of the various problems we need to investigate. His concept of institutionalisation is particularly problematic in this respect. It has at least three distinct meanings in his work – those of orientation towards structured situations, emergence of organisation and approbation by the centre. There need be no necessary connection between these three aspects and it is important to keep them analytically distinct.[21] The present approach distinguishes between social movements in terms of their radicalism, their methods and their degree of derogation or proscription by the centre.[22] We can then examine the impact of organisation on the dynamics of social movements and their legitimisation by the government-and-control apparatus as well as the preference for a variety of methods on their progress and approbation.

Secularisation

Structural differentiation is accompanied by cultural secularisation. On the one hand the value system must be respecified to apply to the various differentiated subsystems and segmental units; on the other hand the value system must be couched at a higher level of generality in order to legitimise the wider variety of goals and functions in these subsystems.[23] This is supposed to result in increased flexibility and adaptability in the culture and in an increased freedom of dissent for the individual actor.[24] Secularisation can be defined then as the process whereby the value system become less rigidly specified and more permissive in its content. This process is clearly relevant to the analysis of social movements – especially the possibilities of a given movement resulting in reform or revolution.

48

It is the normative functionalists who have emphasised this idea most explicitly in their theoretical writings and it is either absent or only implicit in conflict and exchange theories. A major reason for this is surely that the constraint theorists are less interested in the evaluation of dissent and in the cultural system as a whole. They lay far more emphasis on the constraints imposed by differentiated structures – increased interdependence and technological sophistication simply decrease the amount of real freedom in advanced societies. This is apparent not only in the Marcusean concept of the one-dimensional society and its system of repressive tolerance but also in Marx's writing on alienation and political emancipation.[25] Thus Marx argues that the separation of the state from both religious and economic life liberated the *state* from religion and economics but did not liberate *man* from their domination.[26] There is a distinction to be drawn, therefore, between political emancipation and human emancipation – as yet man has received only religious liberty, the liberty to engage in business, the liberty to own property, and not liberation from religion, from business, from property.[27] Structural differentiation replaces personal arbitrariness by impersonal arbitrariness. Although individuals seem freer under the dominance of the bourgeoisie, for example, because their conditions of life seem accidental, they are really less free because they are subject to the constraint of a mode of production free from conscious direction.[28]

This argument is important for a proper understanding of the stability of social order in complex societies. The normative functionalist is quite right in arguing that structural differentiation leads to secularisation and thus to an increase in personal freedom at the cultural level. But consensus becomes less important precisely because structural constraints are increasingly important. The individual is certainly more free to believe and to value what he likes – within the limits set by the need for smooth operation of the differentiated systems and circulating media; but he is also more constrained by the structure of activities and the circulation of generalised media. Thus, while dissent may indeed become easier, actual social change by those outside the societal centre is likely to become more difficult. This apparent paradox will receive greater attention below.

Interests

Marxian sociology distinguishes between the substructure and superstructure of society. This distinction is absent from normative functionalism and exchange theory. Indeed Parsons has argued that it is based on a failure to achieve a high enough level of abstraction with the result that Marxist sociologists are unable to account for the nature of the legal system and the role of cultural traditions in the determination of interests.[29] Only a higher level of abstraction that treats both the material base and the superstructure as particular combinations of the same analytically defined, more generalised variables can deal with such problems.[30] These more generalised variables are those of the components of action – values, norms, collectivities and facilities – which must all be combined to produce social action. The infrastructure, which is the analytical equivalent of Parsons' adaptive functional subsystem, is a complex structure of all four components and is involved in interchanges with the three other functional subsystems. It is therefore fallacious to distinguish between a material substratum and cultural superstructure without also emphasising the essential similarity of their more basic components. This argument is well founded and a synthesis must allow for it.

In the present analysis, therefore, we shall omit the distinction between material base and superstructure as such – a distinction recognised as problematic even by Marxist sociologists[31] – and employ in its place the distinction between economic, political, social and cultural subsystems formulated by the normative functionalists. The relative primacy of the subsystems can be determined either empirically or by means of assumption during the construction of the general theory. Moreover, whatever the relative long-term primacy, there is considerable scope for variation in subsystem dominance in the short-term.[32]

Related to the distinction between material substratum and superstructure is the Marxian notion of interests and the conflict of interests. Interests have always been problematic in sociological theory because of their relativity and the difficulties introduced by the ideological presentation of 'true interests'. Marxist sociology posits a fundamental conflict of interests between capitalists and wage-earners: that is, the existence of bourgeois private property is inimical to the realisation of the interests of wage-earners in the product of their labour. Only the abolition of wage-labour is compatible with the abolition of capitalist exploitation: exploitation is the *sine qua non* of capitalism and, indeed, of all earlier forms of production. Surplus labour is the primary category of interest in classical Marxist sociology and

50

interests are defined in terms of relative control over the product of surplus labour. More generally, interests can be defined in terms of relative opportunities for want-satisfaction and in terms of means to want-satisfaction. Thus something is in one's interests to the extent that it increases one's opportunities for want-satisfaction more than some specified alternative.[33] Logically there are no absolute interests in the sense of things that produce a greater increase in opportunities for want-satisfaction than any other possible alternative for a particular individual or class – for it will always be possible to think of a further alternative which makes the individual or class marginally better off. In the context of specific social structures, however, it may well be possible to define such absolute interests in constant-sum situations: it is absolutely in one's interests to gain the whole sum of whatever is available.[34] But even then the actual social structure may constrain the realisation of such absolute interests and enforce a relative distribution of interests.

While classical Marxist sociologists focus almost exclusively on economic interests (i.e. interests in the product of surplus labour), it is possible to conceive of other interests. The Parsonian categorisation of sanctions provides a useful basis for the classification of interests. Thus we can distinguish among economic interests in the availability of inducements; political interests in control over physical coercion; social interests in the exercise of persuasion; and cultural interests in control over commitments. Such interests can be employed in satisfying a greater or lesser range of wants. There is no necessary connection between the type of interest and the use to which it may be put. Thus an important aspect of the realisation of the proletariat's economic interests is an increase in their control over means of coercion.

The four types of interest are all social interests in the sense that they can be realised only in a social context. Other interests are relevant to isolated individuals (e.g. tools for economic production, weapons for defence against animals). Social interests are clearly dependent on an institutional framework and given normative order. Where there are only sanctions of low generalisation, they will have narrowly circumscribed uses and thus an individual's wants will significantly determine his interests. Where sanctions have attained a high degree of generalisation and symbolisation, an individual's interests will be less determined by his wants – but he will also acquire a set of 'second-order' interests in the stability of the institutional framework and the normative

51

order that make generalised media possible. The extent of such 'second-order' interests will obviously depend on the extent of the individual's actual and expected control over generalised media and on his actual and expected control over more basic sanctions.[35] Where the individual has little control over either symbolic or substantive sanctions, his interests must lie in some kind of redistribution within the system or through a reorganisation of the social structure. In any event discussion of interests cannot be divorced from discussion of institutions and value systems even though interests and values can be distinguished analytically.

In the ensuing synthesis, therefore, we do not employ the distinction between material base and superstructure as such; rather we distinguish between the economic, political, social and cultural subsystems. We do, however, distinguish between interests and values and analyse the complex and manifold interrelations between them. In particular we emphasise the relativity of the interest concept and thus the theoretical possibility of the infinite divisibility of interests. The latter is an important principle for structural analysis and must be counterposed to the logic of dichotomies which sees interests as always dualistic and antithetic. The structure of societies is always complex and so is the distribution of interests. Thus it is essential to distinguish between an individual's interests in a particular situation, his 'second-order' interests in different types of sanction, and his interests in structural reorganisation and redistribution. Likewise it is necessary to analyse the relations between different positions an individual actor occupies in the structural matrix and to compare these relations and positions with those occupied by others. In the following chapter we introduce a framework for the analysis of these and other problems.

Conclusions

In this chapter we have examined a number of joint concerns and emergent themes in structural analysis. Wherever possible we have attempted to combine the analytical insights and assumptions of the different theories; where this has not been possible we have considered the reasons for preferring one or other approach. It should now be apparent that some sort of synthesis between the different theories is possible, based on the themes emphasised in the preceding analysis. We now turn, therefore, to the presentation of an analytical framework that combines the contributions of the different approaches into a unified conceptual system and then attempt to articulate this framework through the postulation of a number of assumptions about structural dynamics.

4 Conceptual Framework

We are now in a position to elaborate a conceptual framework which combines into a coherent whole the particular insights of the three different general theories reviewed in earlier chapters. The synthesis will be presented in the form of a symbolic model of societal structure and its rationale is based on the concepts of power, exchange and institutionalisation. In this chapter we will outline the main analytical elements of the theory – beginning with the structural properties of societal systems and then proceeding to an examination of exchange relations and finally to the analysis of cultural systems. In the next chapter we make a number of assumptions and derive their implications for societal analysis. Thereafter we introduce a number of brief case studies in order, reform and revolution.

Centre and Periphery

Every societal system is a power system. In every society the distribution of power has a determinate structure and in every society this distribution is inegalitarian. The extent of power hierarchisation and the primary bases of power vary from society to society. So also do the recruitment and interrelations of the powerful and the exploitativeness of their rule. And likewise we may observe variation in the nature of their legitimation and the ideals that they strive to attain. Power is the most important aspect of societal structure.[1] But recognition of its importance is quite different from presenting an adequate analytical framework for its examination. In this work the main organising concept in the discussion of societal power relations is the centre-periphery distinction. We consider its dimensions and implications below.

The centre-periphery distinction is not new. It has been employed by Shils, Lerner, Eistenstadt, Lipset and Rokkan, Nettl and Robertson, Stinchcombe, Curry and Wade, and many others.[2] As used in the past, however, it contains certain ambiguities – the most important being a simultaneous emphasis on the centre as a realm of values and as a realm of action;[3] and a circularity in definition – the central values are those espoused

54

by the ruling authorities, the ruling authorities are those whose power is legitimated by central values.[4] Clarification of these ambiguities is essential to the fruitful employment of the distinction in future work.

In this monograph, therefore, *centre* refers to the structural aspect of power and comprises those organisations, groups and individuals (whether incumbents of particular roles or of status-sets which provide a special power potential) who exercise most 'power' in a given social system. Inclusion within the centre depends on the actual exercise of power and not simply, or necessarily, on the normative specification of its exercise. In more differentiated societies it is possible to examine a number of centres based on different types of power – economic, political, social and cultural. Moreover, in certain types of system, such as neo-colonial societies, the centre(s) may include organisations, groups and individuals who are extra-territorial wielders of power. The *periphery* is likewise defined in terms of actual power relations. It comprises those organisations, groups and individual role-incumbents who exercise least 'power' in the society or other system in question. It should be possible to construct centre-periphery continua on the basis of quantitative measures of power and so reduce the apparently residual and arbitrary nature of this distinction.[5] A specification of the actual hierarchies of power and their interrelations will in any case be necessary to provide adequate information about the structure and distribution of different interests in the societal system.

In the cultural sphere we shall refer to the *'central value system'*. It comprises the values, beliefs and symbols publicly espoused by the centre and need not correspond to the actual realities of the situation. In more differentiated societies it may be necessary to distinguish between the central value systems of different centres. Corresponding to the periphery in cultural analysis we find peripheral *subcultures* more or less distinct from the central value system and capable of analysis without reference to it (or them). But where the peripheral value system (or that of any social group) cannot be analysed without reference to central values since it contains as a primary element themes of conflict with and/or opposition to the latter, then we have a *contra-culture*.[6] Clearly the extent of such conflict and opposition themes is variable and the sub- and contra-culture distinction is therefore best treated as a continuum to be related to variations in structural location and to psychocultural factors.

Finally, we may note that the institutionalisation or legitimation of social movements is referred to the central value system. A movement is institutionalised to the extent that its methods and objects are prescribed or preferred in terms of central values and their specification. Conversely, it is uninstitutionalised to the extent that its methods and objects are derogated or proscribed in terms of such values and their specification. Since central value systems are often ill-defined, inconsistent and ambiguous, there will often be doubts as to the legitimacy of a given social movement. Such ambiguities are often reflected in inconsistent reactions on the part of different types and levels of central organisations and individuals; and in strategies such as the development of a dual structure – open and underground – on the part of social movements. Thus the degree of institutionalisation is not just an analytical problem but also an empirical problem faced by social movements and central powers alike.

Further analysis and description of the centre-periphery distinction is clearly dependent on a more refined analysis of power and exchange relations. In the following paragraphs we elaborate an analytical framework for their investigation. In so doing we shall also be able to give a more rounded interpretation to the notion of social structure in terms of the actually obtaining patterns of equality and inequality in control over persons and facilities and in exchange transactions between both equals and unequals.

The Bases of Power Relations

Power is a generic term[7] for the ability of a given social actor (individual or collective) to constrain another actor (or actors) to do something that he (or they) would not otherwise do.[8] The basis of such power may be control over situational or intentional, positive or negative sanctions. Thus the essence of a power situation is that the powerful can manipulate either the situation and/or intentions so that the less powerful will prefer compliance with the wishes of the powerful to non-compliance. Whether or not the less powerful will in fact comply with such wishes is dependent not only on the type of sanctions controlled by the more powerful but also on the preference structures of the less powerful.[9] Theoretically the latter can always choose to forgo inducements, submit to coercion, resist persuasion and deny commitments. That they do not do so in practice is a necessary condition of the exercise of power in such situations.

It is in this sense that power relations are often called 'zero-sum' relations. But it should be emphasised that to define power in this way and to label it a 'zero-sum' phenomenon is *not* also to say that any power relation necessarily involves continuous opposition to the powerful from the less powerful (a 'basic force' situation[10]) *nor* that the powerful always exercise power to the latter's disadvantage. All that is usually implied by this concept is that there is a hierarchy of power and that, should the powerful wish to exercise their power, the less powerful would be unable to resist them – certainly in the short term and, in the absence of force depletion through the exercise of power, also in the longer term. Basic force situations are rare in any society. Much more common are situations in which actors employ their power resources intermittently rather than continuously: there is a potential for opposition or domination that is occasionally realised and at other times co-operation or competition are normal.[11] It is only on the assumption that a plurality of actors in a given power relation individually seek to maximise control over others that there is a necessary and inevitable conflict in that relationship. To the extent that actors seek only to maximise their rewards, to optimise their power, or simply to satisfy some lower level expectations for rewards or power, then there is scope for co-operation as well as conflict. If we are to gain an adequate understanding of the dynamics of power relations we must therefore examine the determinants of variation in the preference for different degrees and combinations of power and rewards.

The nature and extent of power are clearly variable and multidimensional, and this raises further problems of analysis. At a minimum it is necessary to distinguish among the type of sanctions controlled, the numbers that can be constrained, the scope of activities that can be constrained, the costs of power and of noncompliance, and the amount of constraint exercised (i.e. the probability that an actor would act as he did minus the probability that he would have done so prior to the exercise of power).[12] At present there is no way of combining these different aspects of power into a single indicator of power. Indeed it is difficult, especially in non-experimental situations, to produce reliable measurements of some aspects at all. For macroscopic analyses, however, even limited information, especially when combined with knowledge about command over power bases, is sufficient to give an *indication* of the crucial power relations.

We follow Parsons' analysis of sanctions in our classification

57

of the types of power. We thus distinguish between four main types of power – economic, military or political, social and cultural. Within this general framework we may say that the ultimate basis of economic power is control over the means of production, distribution and exchange of goods and services; that of political power is control over the means of coercion; that of social power is control over the means of status attribution; and that of cultural power is control over the means of value creation, interpretation and maintenance. In addition to these ultimate or primary bases of power, there are four main types of secondary base. These are quite simply the products (outputs) of each primary base : goods and services, physical force, status and value commitments. It is these that correspond to the four Parsonian sanctions of inducement, coercion, persuasion or contingent acceptance, and the activation of commitments. Lastly, under certain structural and cultural conditions, tertiary bases of power may develop and become institutionalised. These are the symbolic media of money, authorisation,[13] influence and generalised commitments. Such media have no value-in-use and their value-in-exchange is dependent on their acceptance and institutionalisation by the centre. Apart from money, however, these media are little developed and certainly far from generalised even in highly differentiated societies. Authorisation, influence and generalised commitments are more closely tied to particular roles and uses and more restricted in scope than is true of money. Thus authorisation and influence generally operate within hierarchical institutional contexts and even *generalised* commitments must be integrated with central values.[14]

This fourfold classification of power is clearly analytical rather than empirical. Allowing for the distinction between primary, secondary and tertiary resources, it can be shown to cover a wide variety of empirically conceivable power bases. Power can be exercised in various ways : through exercising one's control over the different ultimate power bases and thus altering the structure of opportunities (e.g. closing a factory in a one-company town), through employment of secondary resources, or through use of more generalised media of exchange. The relative efficacy of the four types and levels of power will vary with the uses to which they are put and the preference structures of the less powerful. These in turn will vary with the social structure, socialisation experience and the development of contracultures.

There is no necessary correspondence between the different

types of power such that, for example, economic power is invariably associated with determinate degrees of control over other possible power bases. That is to say, the four types of power are *analytically independent* and thus imply the possibility of inconsistency or incongruence between positions on different power hierarchies. The analytical independence of these types of power involves not only the actual exercise of power but also the channels of recruitment for each power hierarchy. Empirically it is thus necessary to examine not only the interconnections between power élites but also the patterns of recruitment and criteria of promotion within each hierarchy.

While it may seem peculiar to talk of social and cultural bases of power analogous to the economic 'substratum', it is important to realise that status and commitments are also produced and that there is a determinate pattern of control over the means by which they are produced. It is thus essential to distinguish analytically between the *nature of the end-product* and the *means whereby it is produced*. This distinction is especially important where these means are primarily material in nature (e.g. mass communications) and thus dependent on the economy for their production and the polity for their protection. Where status attribution and value creation are dependent primarily on the performance of the actors in specified roles the distinction is empirically less important but none the less crucial at the analytical level. It is in these terms, for example, that we may contrast the monarch as fount of honour and the priest as cultural interpreter with the pecuniary status system and the modern mass media. Yet those who have power over the monarch or priest in their roles have the same type of power as those who control the distribution of consumer goods or the content of the mass media.[15]

The four power bases can also be considered in terms of both their forces and relations of production in way analogous to the more general treatment of the material base in Marxist sociology. In this context the 'forces of production' refer to the material and social technology of production and include the division of labour or organisation of production;[16] the 'relations of production' refer to the pattern of control over the total productive process and the pattern of appropriation of the product. The same forces of production can be combined with different relations of production to provide different modes of production. Thus it is possible to have a particular means of status attribution

59

controlled in different ways and for different ends (e.g. contest versus sponsored mobility in educational systems[17]) and particular means of value creation and interpretation subject to different patterns of control (e.g. authoritarian, paternal or commercial patterns in mass communications).[18] It is also possible to discuss contradictions between the forces and relations of production in each ultimate power base. Thus a change in military technology may require larger, national armies but where central power is dependent on the monopoly of coercive apparatus, then such armies may remain unorganised even at the expense of national autonomy.[19] Similarly, where education is a significant means of status attribution, educational innovations will be resisted by the socially prestigious where they would result in an overall up-grading of the educational status of the population at the expense of the higher status of the centre.[20]

We have now completed our preliminary review of the nature and bases of power and therefore turn now to a more detailed – although still far from exhaustive – analysis of these different power bases and the way in which they are organised. We begin this analysis by a consideration of the structure and processes in the economy and then proceed to a discussion of the polity, the status system and the societal value system.

The Economy

Economic power is relatively non-problematic in comparison with other bases of power. It refers ultimately to control over the means of production, distribution and exchange of goods and services; more immediately, it refers to control over such goods and services and to purchasing power. Thus the economic system includes all institutions, organisations and actors in so far as they are concerned with the production, distribution and exchange of goods and services. In our analysis of economic systems we are concerned primarily with their institutional structure, their dynamics and their interrelations with other societal systems. We are not concerned with the development of models of rational behaviour in different types of market situation. Economic rationality or economising behaviour (whether in budgetary management or the organisation of production) is a contingent rather than necessary attribute of economic action in our sense. The increasing primacy of such rationality, its connections with the development of money and its ramifications on other societal systems are none the less clearly significant in differentiated societies and should be considered in a more detailed work.[21]

The means of production, distribution and exchange can be analysed in terms of the well-known distinctions between land, labour, capital and enterprise. There are four broad classes corresponding to control over these different means of economic activity – land-owners, labourers, capitalists and entrepreneurs. These classes will be differentiated into narrower interest groups through variation in such factors as the marginality and size of landholdings, in the skill and marketability of labour, in the type and amount of capital, and in the nature of entrepreneurial abilities. The combination of such means controlled by different actors will also vary and thus further differentiate the economic class structure of society. Likewise, in the secondary and tertiary sectors of the economy,[22] there will be considerable differentiation in both the amount and type of goods and services and also in the amount and liquidity of money controlled by different economic actors. In addition there is the possibility of conflicts between economic positions in the primary, secondary, and tertiary power systems. Thus individuals with identical sources of income may be divided on the basis of income level when it comes to questions of direct taxation levied on gross or net income. Indirect taxation may also unite persons with similar consumption interests who are divided in terms of other economic interests.[23] In short, it is arbitrary to assert on *a priori* grounds that economic classes are necessarily dichotomous and antagonistic in their interests. Any realistic assessment of economic class structures, especially in more complex societies, must recognise the differentiation and variety of economic interests. The extent to which any given economic interest or class pattern becomes dominant must be treated as contingent and dependent on the dynamics of the economy and its manifold interrelations with other systems.

It is none the less possible to point to one or two fundamental points of conflict in the economy. Thus, while in an expanding economy the amount of goods and services and of money income can be treated as variable, the distribution of control over the primary means of production is always a fixed-sum relation. Although it is logically and empirically possible for labourers to gain an increase in real income without loss to other classes, therefore, it is still impossible for them to gain an increase in real power over the total productive process without a concomitant

61

loss to others. The extent to which workers can gain control over factory management and investment decisions, for example, is dependent on the extent to which such control is ceded by the other classes or interest groups in the relevant economic system.[24] Thus the ultimate basis of power provides a more radical and antagonistic basis of conflict than does the distribution of control over either goods and services or real money income. It is control over productive property that structures the most radical and antagonistic latent classes. Related to this consideration is the problem of the relative dominance of different forces and relations of production in a given economy. Where new modes of production are becoming dominant, for example, there will be a fundamental conflict of interest between those whose power is based on control over the increasingly subordinate bases of power and those who control the newly emergent or newly dominant mode of production wherever the two groups of controllers are distinct. Where the old economic dominants move into the new mode of production and control, of course, such conflict is largely absent. Thirdly, where the economy is not expanding, then conflict over the distribution of the economic product can also become the basis for radical conflicts – chronic in less developed subsistence economies, acute in static or declining industrial societies.[25] In short, economic conflict tends to be most radical and antagonistic in character where it concerns power relations and resources that are not subject to expansion; where it concerns expandable resources, it is less radical and more accommodative in character.

It should be clear, therefore, that any analysis of economic class relations and class conflict must be conducted in the light of the pattern of economic change and not on the assumption of a static economy. It is changes in the type and degree of economic power that affect the dynamics of economic relations as much as, if not more than, the pattern at any given moment in time. Thus we cannot afford to ignore the dynamics of economies under different modes of production and different social, political and cultural constraints in our analysis of order, reform and revolution. The level of structural differentiation, the differential participation of economic classes in the political system, the criteria of status attribution, the relative emphases of the cultural system and many other non-economic factors affect the development of the economy, the pattern of class conflict and the relative institutionalisation of such conflict. A more detailed analysis of these problems and their effects must await the exposition of the structure of the social, political and cultural systems.

The Polity

Political power is more problematic than economic power. It refers ultimately to control over the means of physical coercion but includes much more on other levels. The development of political institutions based on authority rather than the immediate application, or threat of application, of physical violence creates fundamental problems in the analysis of political power systems. It is important to distinguish between authority and cultural power in this respect. Whereas the primary focus of responsibility for the implementation of value commitments is the individual, in the polity this responsibility is placed on authorities who must back up their commands with force if necessary. Where the 'authorities' are unable to support their commands with force if and when required, they will be rendered ineffectual.[26] None the less authority and authorisation do depend on acceptance of values and norms defining the legitimacy and scope of authority; and an emergent normative order is a major feature of the breakthrough from basic force situations to more stable political systems. Ultimately, however, it is the distribution of control over the means of coercion that defines the distribution of political power. Authority without coercive power is liable to displacement and it is to reinforce and support their authority that states everywhere attempt to establish and maintain a monopoly over the means of coercion within their territorial domain.

It is thus necessary to examine the distribution of control over the means of coercion in order to understand the dynamics of power systems. Control over military equipment and remuneration and the level of military technology are of fundamental importance in this respect. If a military élite controls complex military equipment and remunerates the rank-and-file personnel, it is comparatively easy for it to coerce the periphery and to maintain an inequitable distribution of resources through political means. If the level of military technology is low and the rank-and-file personnel provide their own weaponry, such coercion and such distributions are more difficult to implement.[27] Control over capital military equipment must be combined, however, with military organisation or military skills to be effective. It is therefore also necessary to examine the relations between those who control the equipment and remuneration of the military and those who organise and lead military forces.[28] Civilian control of the military – especially where the military and non-military centres are distinct – is always problematic and must be reinforced by non-political means if it is to be successfully maintained.[29] Other sources of conflict in the military system are to be found in the relations between different sectors or types of military organisation (e.g. air, land and sea forces, or regular, police and secret police forces); and over the distribution of protection, or the incidence of violence, in society.[30] Thus it is control over the means of coercion, the uses to which they are put and the relative dominance of different technologies of violence that provide the major sources of 'military class conflict'.

We now turn to an examination of authority structures and their relevance to the political system. It is important to note that authority is of course strongly institutionalised in most military organisations and that the absence of authority and its concomitant discipline considerably weakens military effectiveness. Authority becomes politically important and distinctive, however, when it acquires a non-military primacy. Political authority may be relatively informal and non-hierarchical, as in primitive bands and segmentary societies, but in more differentiated societies it tends to become formally organised and hierarchical.[31] Such institutions as centralised or federative monarchies, feudal estates, legislative assemblies and government bureaucracies[32] are clearly dependent on such formalised authority structures. In any authority system there is a fundamental distinction between those who wield authority and those who are subject to it. This distinction may become manifested in radical, antagonistic 'authority class' conflict between the authorities and their subordinates.[33] Moreover, in more complex and formalised systems, there is often a real distinction between those who control the means of authorisation, those who organise the authority system and those who work at subordinate levels in the system. These distinctions are also associated with conflicts of interest and may develop into open conflict. Lastly, it is also necessary to examine the potential and actual conflicts over the determination of what is to be authorised and over the distribution of costs and benefits in its implementation. Such conflicts typically involve those outside the authority system and involve the use of non-political sanctions as well as military and authoritative constraints. An investigation of such policy conflict thus involves consideration of other power systems as well as the internal structure and dynamics of the political system. We now turn, therefore, to the last two types of power system : the status and cultural systems.

The Status System

Social power is based on control over the means of status attribution. Status is generally thought to be grounded in the membership of valued collectivities or the occupancy of valued roles in the economic, political, social or cultural systems. Social power can therefore be redefined in terms of differential control over access to such collectivities and roles. Such power is thus both a crucial aspect of social stratification systems and of social structure in general.[34]

In at least one respect, therefore, social power is dependent on the predefinition of valued positions. But this no more means that social power is reducible to cultural power than the dependence of economic power on protection of productive property, or the dependence of political power on economic production of the means of coercion and on cultural legitimation, makes one reducible to the other. Rather does this point to the interdependence of the different bases of power and different types of power system. However, interdependence implies not only the possibility of equality of influence between systems or persons, but also the possibility of differential influence or autonomy. The relative autonomy of different systems is an important variable in comparative analysis and it is rare that the status system is the most autonomous system owing to its dependence on cultural power.

Those who control status attribution establish the terms and routes of entry into valued collectivities and roles for different economic, political, social and cultural classes. The terms of entry may vary from purely ascriptive criteria, such as age, sex or genealogical descent, to achieved criteria, such as educational attainment, military prowess and entrepreneurial ability. Terms of entry may well vary for different status aspirants so that the more peripheral the individual, the more resources he must sacrifice in the quest for upward mobility.[35] The translation of high status or esteem within subcollectivities into macrosocietal influence will likewise be subject to control by those with social power. Where access to valued positions and collectivities is determined by purely ascriptive criteria, whether genealogical descent or age-grade, influence is also likely to be based on esteem within the society or its subgroups. Thus in so-called 'unstratified' societies, in which there is institutionalised equality of access to positions of power, there is none the less scope for the exercise of influence based on other qualities or performances – whether secular or supernatural.[36] Social power, in the sense of control over status attribution, is certainly weak in comparison with other societies; but influence is a significant mode of constraint on fellow members of such a society.

The fundamental basis of conflict within the stratification system is control over the terms and routes of entry to valued roles and collectivities. Thus competing bases of status and competition for control over a given basis of status attribution provide the main source of such conflict. In contrast with other secondary bases of power, moreover, status is inherently a fixed-sum resource : an increase in the proportion of actors with a given status automatically 'devalues' that status and its potential for influence. Those with a given status thus have a strong interest in controlling access to their stratum and are vulnerable to attempts by the social centre to expand their numbers and so undermine their influence base as well as other advantages they may enjoy. Such attempts at control will usually involve the employment of non-social resources and constraints and thus generate broader conflicts extending beyond the stratification system.[37]

It should be emphasised that status is a relationship and involves deference as a concomitant. Without such deference status is meaningless and attempts at influence are bound to be ineffective. The directly interpersonal nature of status relationships is conducive to the emergence of status consciousness and thereby contributes to the aggravation of status conflicts. The existence of multiple bases of status creates further problems in this respect owing to the possibility of incongruency between positions in different status hierarchies. Thus in contacts between a professional worker from a low-status ethnic minority and an unskilled manual worker from a high-status ethnic group there is a potential conflict over their relative status and deference positions. Such conflict is most likely to emerge where comparative status is relevant to the interaction and may well be absent in cases of mutual attraction and economic or political interdependence. Where comparative status is salient through time and the

66

status inconsistent cannot equilibrate their status positions, they may support or organise movements to change the terms of status attribution and the institutions that define status.[38] Conflict based on such movements is especially likely where the status inconsistency is derived from power incongruency, that is, from imbalances in economic, political, social and cultural power.

Status is also the basis for persuasion and influence. These operate through the offer of good reasons why, independently of situational advantages that the person exercising influence or persuasion may provide, it would be a good thing to act in a particular way. Persuasion and influence are most important where both situational advantages and normative commitments are uncertain, ambiguous or even absent. In such circumstances individuals may turn to those with high status or esteem for advice as to an appropriate course of action. Thus they differ from the activation of commitments in that they typically operate where norms are weak and they can be used to convey support and cognitive as well as evaluative beliefs. These cognitive beliefs define the situation and may include statements about situational advantages and disadvantages as well as normative and expressive considerations. Influence and persuasion are thus important in many situations and can become the basis for conflicting definitions of the situation and for appeal to different status criteria in justifying acceptance of one of these definitions.

Where status is based on incumbency of particular positions within a collectivity or is associated with a more diffuse deferential following, it can become the basis of influence or persuasion not only in the group or following but also outside. Thus an actor with high status – whether economic, political, social or cultural in origin – may use this position to mobilise support for outsiders in exchange for substantive rewards for himself and/or his group or following. Conversely those who wish to influence a particular collectivity can do so by constraining the activities of a 'middle-man' with prestige in that group or following. In this way status and influence become important means of articulating complex and highly differentiated societies and ensuring their flexibility – although this is by no means guaranteed by the existence of stratification.

Status attribution and its concomitant persuasion and influence operate within a normative framework that defines the relative worth of different roles and collectivities. The economy and polity are similarly dependent on such a framework for legitima-

67

tion and regulation of their activities. Inducements, coercion and persuasion can in turn be employed to constrain the operation of the cultural system. It is to an examination of the latter system – in many respects the key system in any society – that we now turn.

The Cultural Power System

Cultural power is based on control over the means of value creation, interpretation and maintenance. Whatever the origins of a given value its importance depends on its successful transmission and maintenance through diffusion and socialisation processes of one kind or another. It must also be interpreted and specified in particular contexts if it is to be effective in determining behaviour in a wide range of contexts.

Control over the content of the societal value system is in the interests of every member of the society. Yet it is generally those with power in other systems rather than those without such power who exercise cultural power. These other centres need the justification and regulation provided by the cultural system; and they need the various types of commitment – contingent and non-contingent – that it can create. Values and norms are important precisely because the power relationship is contingent on the preference structures of the less powerful as well as the resources available to the more powerful members of a given system. It is inherent in the power relation that the less powerful may decide to forgo inducements, submit to coercion, resist persuasion or deny commitments. The ability to prevent such contingencies through the determination of the choices made by the less powerful is thus especially critical to the operation of other power bases. The creation of commitments to economic, political, social or cultural activities that are not contingent on a continuing supply of substantive rewards is of particular interest to each power centre since it ensures at least a minimum level of system operation and also frees rewards for other uses.[39] If a given centre can also develop commitments to its own rather than another type of reward, its power is further increased through control over contingent activities. Conversely, to the extent that a peripheral group can create commitments to particular values among the economic, political or social centres, then it can control the operation of these systems in its own interests. Approximations to such a situation can be found in civilian control of the military through cultural commitments to a subordinate

68

professional role determined by civilian authorities; and in political systems where the government is committed to the interests of the whole society and not just to those of its more powerful supporters.[40]

The fundamental base of conflict in the cultural system is differential control over the means of value creation and interpretation. Thus the critical point in the development of cultural systems is the emergence, for whatever reason, of specialised cultural roles and collectivities.[41] In less differentiated societies culture is emergent and consensual and cultural power, although by no means completely absent, is diffuse and limited in scope. As structural differentiation proceeds to fragment interests there is an increase in conflict over the institutionalisation and interpretation of values. Different interest groups develop competing interpretations of dominant values and attempt to impose new values on other relevant groups. In such conflicts it is often not only control over cultural resources (e.g. literacy, mass media) but also control over other power bases that leads to success. The periphery is thus normally unable to impose its own values, even where these are adequate to the situation, without support from more powerful groups or individuals. The development of complex cultural 'technologies' thus combines with increasing power hierarchisation to create the possibility of a social order based on ideological hegemony rather than physical repression.[42]

In addition to conflict over the control of a given means of value creation, there will be conflict between those who control different 'means of mental production'. Cultural conflict between state and religious organisations is an oft-cited example of such antagonism. Moreover, where cultural technologies are complex and highly organised, there is likely to develop conflict – as in other formal organisations – between those who own, those who organise and those who work at subordinate levels within a cultural organisation. Universities in Western capitalist societies provide a contemporary illustration of both fundamental and organisational conflict in the cultural system : the economic, political and social centres are interested in the content and beneficiaries of education and thereby aggravate the conflicts over the distribution of power inside the university.

We have now completed our brief examination of the different power systems and shortly turn to a consideration of the exchange relations that emerge from differential control over power bases. Although this examination has focused on four analytically separate power systems, it should be emphasised that these systems are empirically interdependent and interpenetrating. The operation of the judicial system exemplifies such interlocking of different power systems. Simultaneously the judiciary often interprets norms, authorises coercion, allocates economic costs and rewards and undermines or reinforces status. Its operation is dependent on the support of the political and cultural systems, the economy and the social system. In turn it affects the operation of all four systems. Many other roles and organisations are similarly interstitial or intermediate in significance – mediating between different systems and/or combining several types of power in their operation. A more detailed analysis would have to consider not only relatively 'pure' types of power structure but also these impure types. But we must now move on to a consideration of exchange relations and postpone such analyses to the case studies of social order and disorder.

Exchange and Exploitation

In preceding sections we have considered the nature of power and the different bases of power in any social system. Control over a power base is not to be confused, however, with the actual employment of resources in social interaction. An individual with great potential power may in fact choose not to realise that potential or may do so to the advantage rather than detriment of the less powerful. Power is an emergent relationship that depends on the actual employment of resources in attempts to constrain other actors and on the compliance of those others with the wishes of the powerful. It is thus necessary to examine not only the distribution of control over different power resources but also the ways in which such control and resources are employed in various exchange relations.

Exchange and power are twin aspects of interaction. Power refers to the ability to constrain other actors to do something they would not otherwise do. Exchange refers to the balance of rewards and costs for each participant in the interaction. Both the interaction between centre and periphery and the interaction between different power systems can be analysed in terms of power and exchange relations and it is important to distinguish between these two aspects. The distinction is particularly important because of the long-term impact of exchange relations on the balance of power and on the probability of social disorder.

An exploitative power system increases power hierarchisation while a beneficial power system reduces centre-periphery differentiation.[43] Likewise an exploitative system is likely to provoke disorder and reaction whereas a beneficial system is likely to promote social order and harmony. In the following discussion we first introduce definitions of exploitation, reciprocity and benefaction; and then examine the exchange relations between different power systems and different centres and their peripheries.

The balance of rewards and costs ('profits'[44]) can in principle vary from exploitation through reciprocity to benefaction. Exploitation occurs where the more powerful gain disproportionately from their contributions to the interaction; reciprocity occurs where the rewards are directly proportional to costs; and benefaction occurs where the more powerful gain less than proportionately from their contributions. Proportionality can be variously defined in terms of absolute objective, relative objective or subjective standards. An absolute objective standard is possible in principle and would involve a standard unit of contribution as a baseline; in practice such a measure would be difficult to develop and operationalise.[45] A relative objective standard is easier to develop and would involve comparison of 'profit' rates with the average rate for the power system in question : those individuals or organisations making more than a given amount above the average would be considered exploitative, those making below average profits beneficial.[46] Lastly subjective measures would be based on participants' beliefs about the relative balance of costs and rewards. The most useful approach would obviously involve the theoretical and empirical linkage of both relative objective and subjective measures for the analysis of proportionality in power hierarchisation and dissent.

We have already noted that differentiated power systems are none the less interdependent. This interdependence consists in the exchange of secondary and tertiary resources between systems so that each can produce its own secondary and tertiary resources. Thus the economy produces goods and services for the other power systems and these goods and services are then combined with other resources to produce coercion and policy benefits, status and value commitments. In return the economy receives protection and policy benefits from the polity, status and influence from the status system, and more or less specific commitments to economic activity and institutions from the cultural system. There are similar exchanges between other systems.

71

While the economy and status systems acquire their inputs primarily through the exchange of positive resources, the political and cultural systems must initially acquire their inputs through a negative exchange. Later, however, even the polity and cultural system are able to offer positive advantages in return for inputs from other systems – policy benefits and commitments to non-cultural activities and institutions. There is thus an apparent asymmetry in the exchange potential of the different power systems. The economy and status systems are based on control over positive sanctions and can thus achieve a surplus in their exchange relations with other systems. Conversely the political and cultural systems are based on control over negative sanctions and a surplus is less easily achieved or, indeed, identifiable. By taking our analysis back to the ultimate power bases of each system, however, we see that in all four cases a surplus involves non-employment of means of production, coercion, status attribution or value creation. These are then released for production, consumption or exchange in other contexts. A strong centre is thus able to engage in conspicuous consumption and the accumulation of its own means of production rather than expend its output in acquiring the inputs of other systems. It is also able to employ the surplus either in developing other bases of power and thereby increasing its autonomy; or in reducing the level of exploitation in its own system and thereby decreasing the likelihood of peripheral dissent. Any of the four systems is capable of being the strong centre but there are obviously different conditions for maintaining the strength of each system. Technological development and other dynamic factors are likely to reinforce or undermine these conditions and so change the dominant institutions and values of society.[47]

Exchanges between centre and periphery occur whatever the level of intersystemic differentiation. Any examination of these exchanges must avoid identifying a particular concrete group or class with either the centre or the periphery. Such an identification can be made only on empirical grounds after analytical delineation of the nature of centre and periphery. The centre can be defined in terms of its differential control over the production and distribution of resources and the periphery in terms of its subjection to and dependence on such control. The centre employs such control to acquire the inputs it needs not only from other systems but also from the peripheral members of its own system. Whereas the centre is motivated by a desire not only for rewards but also for control over the bases of power, the periphery is perforce motivated primarily by its desire for positive rewards and/or the avoidance of sanctions. In exchange for its various contributions to the different power systems the periphery receives the product of the relevant system. Thus the economic periphery is rewarded by goods and services (or their monetary equivalent); the political periphery is rewarded by the absence of coercion and by policy benefits; the social periphery is rewarded by contingent approval and benefits from the exercise of influence beyond and on behalf of the group; and the cultural periphery is rewarded by a clear conscience and by integrity on the part of the centre.[48] Cases of non-compliance are sanctioned correspondingly – the periphery is denied goods and services, is subjected to coercion, is derogated by centre and deferential periphery and is subject to guilt and public admonitions.[49]

The maximum possible reward for the periphery over a given period is clearly the total product of the relevant system over the same period.[50] The minimum possible reward is that required to maintain the contributions of the periphery for the duration of this period. Exploitation is total at this minimum, therefore, and is reduced to the extent that rewards rise above this level.[51] Any rewards beyond the level of total exploitation are potentially available for investment rather than consumption by members of the periphery and could thus be used to reduce their dependence on the centre for rewards. The degree to which such a potential is realised depends not only on the orientations of the periphery but also on the investment activities of the centre and the tightness of its control over the system. As long as exploitation or monopoly continues, therefore, it is impossible for the periphery to displace the centre or reduce its power through investment of sanctions and resources internal to the system in question. Such goals could still be obtained, however, through other types of power and sanctions (e.g. political action to transfer power in the economy) controlled by a periphery.

While there is a clear analytical correspondence between a given form of compliance and its reward, it is impossible fully to realise this in actual exchange relations. The continuing interpenetration of power systems and the differential strength of centres ensure that any contribution also involves a measure of compliance with other systems. In an undifferentiated society exchanges are necessarily multi-dimensional and compliance is rewarded with a variety of sanctions.[52] As power hierarchisation

73

replaces segmentation in such societies, both exploitation and distortion of rewards become possible. Thus a strong military and economic centre can exploit labour through a distorted emphasis on coercive sanctions; while a strong social and cultural centre can motivate economic services through public approbation and value commitments.[53] The increasing differentiation of control between systems (not to be confused with increasing division of labour within a power system) permits a more accurate correspondence between contribution and reward; but never eliminates distortion entirely.

A useful illustration of the main points made so far about exchange systems is found in Andreski's analysis of the parasitic involution of capitalism. This refers to the tendency to seek profits and to alter market conditions through political means ranging from banditry to the use of state institutions to inhibit union organisation and economic competition. He argues that capitalism will be productive and progressive where entrepreneurs can neither use coercion for parasitic exploitation nor themselves be exploited owing to weakness. Such a situation requires a certain degree of differentiation and segregation between the business and political centres so that money cannot buy everything and coercion cannot be employed with impunity. Latin-American society lacks such an 'equipendency' of business and political centres and politics thus provides a profitable field of investment. Coercion and graft are used to control economic competition and the periphery and there is thus considerable exploitation and distortion. Where the state is weak it cannot be exploitative and does not present profitable opportunities for economic investment. Britain since the fall of the Stuarts provides such a political and economic system. Conversely, where the state is strong and controlled by a non-capitalist class, it is again difficult to use the state for capitalist exploitation. Two examples here are the military-bureaucratic societies of Japan and Imperial Germany.[54] Thus we see that the extent of power differentiation, the relative strength of centres and the exploitation of the periphery are linked in significant respects; and that an adequate understanding of the dynamic tendencies of any society requires attention to all three factors.

Just as we were forced to neglect the importance of interpenetration in our analysis of power systems, so too have we neglected the significance of variations in the nature of the centre-periphery continuum in this section. The present account is most relevant

74

to dichotomous systems in which a monopolistic centre is confronted by a weak and homogeneous periphery. In actual societies this situation is rarely found and there is considerable internal differentiation and gradation within any power system. This gradation and its concomitant pattern of intermediate classes is the precondition of *marginality* in a power system. A marginal individual or organisation is one with considerable nominal power but which none the less receives little return from its resources owing to one or more external constraints. The latter may be due to the increasing power of other individuals or organisations, to the loss of markets for its outputs, to the loss of markets for its inputs, or to some other factor. The marginal person or organisation may itself be exploitative but its exploitation does not generate an adequate return to guarantee continuing power. The marginal businessman, the genteel poor, the unemployed intellectual, younger sons of the nobility, are all examples of marginal individuals. We shall see in fact that such marginal individuals and organisations are important sources of radical dissent and that they can provide support for both innovative and traditionalistic movements.

In the preceding analysis of social structure we often had need to mention properties of interaction not recognised as such by those who participate in the system. Cultural analysis helps alleviate these necessary abstractions through its emphasis on the examination of the actual beliefs, emotions and values that motivate and guide action. We now turn to consider these orientations and their various properties.

Culture Systems

In our analysis of culture we have so far considered only the cultural power system and not the content of the values and norms controlled and interpreted through that system. In this section we examine culture content – the orientations of different actors in society. These orientations may be primarily cognitive, expressive or evaluative and they are important for two main reasons. They provide the meanings of action and thus control over orientations is control over action. And they have emergent properties that are significant *sui generis* determinants of action. These two reasons correspond to two types of causal connection between culture and behaviour. There can be a more or less straightforward connection between individual orientations and action – thus an individual who accepts the central value system may well vote for a party identified with that value system.[55] Secondly, it is possible for the emergent cultural properties (e.g. institutional integration and consensus) to be linked to behaviour – thus a bimodal distribution of opinions on a particular issue may lead to violent conflict between attitude groups.[56] Culture thus enters fundamentally into the analysis of order and change and cannot be excluded from our theory.

There are several ways of analysing the content of orientations: of these pattern variable analysis is the most familiar and most abstract.[57] More important and interesting from our point of view, however, are the degree of radicalism and the level of secularisation. The latter refers to the relative rigidity of normative interpretations or specifications of culture. A secular culture is one in which such specification is flexible and determined primarily by less central organisations and individuals in the light of the various exigencies and constraints that confront them. Conversely a 'sacred' culture is one characterised by moral absolutism – values are precisely specified, action is imbued with heavy moral significance, and deviance is severely sanctioned. Secularisation is significant because it permits the institutionalisation of any dissent that can be presented as an extension or reinterpretation of dominant values. Conversely, sacred cultures not only proscribe dissent but in many cases also prohibit innovations intended to strengthen traditional institutions.[58]

Cultural secularisation accompanies structural differentiation. The latter is possible only where the value system is respecified at a higher level of generality to legitimate the new structures and such respecification encourages in its turn the further differentiation of the system. However, when a single centre institutes the differentiation process and retains control over the new structures, secularisation is less likely to occur and dissent will still be proscribed. Such 'compressed structural differentiation'[59] is often found in developing societies and especially in so-called one-party totalitarian states. Control is retained because the centre lacks trust in the commitment of less powerful organisations and individuals to the dominant values and therefore denies them the opportunity of autonomous interpretation and implementation.

Secularisation is the precondition of the generalisation of commitments such that individuals and organisations obtain this freedom of interpretation. But it also permits increasing apathy

76

towards central values and thus a decline in system performance. Such a decline is likely to provoke a deflationary cycle in which there is a fundamental insistence on the manner of interpretation and distrust of the individual's commitment to implement this interpretation. Secularisation may also lead to cultural inflation in which there is an 'over-commitment' to diverse values so that they cannot be fully implemented owing to situational exigencies or external constraints. Thus secularisation not only confers potential benefits (liberalisation and individual autonomy) but also involves potential disadvantages (apathy, fundamentalism and commitment inflation). Whether benefits or disadvantages are realised is clearly important for social order and social justice.

Radicalism is the other major variable for the analysis of culture content. It refers to the level of social structure or culture to which an individual or organisation is oriented. In the analysis of social movements, therefore, it refers to the level of social structure or culture that a movement seeks to reconstitute or retain. Thus a concern with the distribution of secondary resources is less radical than a concern with the distribution of control over the ultimate bases of power; and a concern with the respecification of a given value is less radical than a concern to replace that value. The degree of radicalism is associated with variations in the combination of power and rewards preferred by different actors. Movements involving persons who are initially interested mainly in rewards are less likely to be radical than those mobilising persons interested in power rather than rewards. Thus trade-union-conscious movements are less radical than politically class-conscious movements. In determining the likely degree of radicalism we need to refer not only to the structure of power within the relevant power systems but also to the effectiveness of central control over the cultural system and to the level of secularisation in the dominant culture. Where cultural power is effective and the culture is secular even fundamental strains in a system may not lead to radical movements. Where hegemonic control is ineffective and the culture sacred even moderate strains can generate an escalation of the level of social structure to be reconstituted.

The two most important emergent properties of culture systems are institutional integration and consensus. *Institutional integration* refers to the consistency of the different dominant value systems, the compatibility between the central economic, political, social and cultural values. *Consensus* refers to the average level and intensity of commitment to different values.[60] Social order requires the commitment of all those with power to disrupt the system and is thus dependent on both consensus and institutional integration. But the greater the structural differentiation and power hierarchisation, the less the need for consensus and the more the need for institutional integration.[61] For in complex hierarchical systems it is primarily other power centres that have disruptive potential, whereas in less complex and more egalitarian societies such a potential characterises the whole population. Thus consensus is most important in relatively undifferentiated and/or egalitarian societies, while in other societies all that is required of the periphery is a pragmatic acquiescence in the *status quo*. The amount and scope of support from other centres is thus critical to the success of peripheral dissent against a given power centre in complex, inegalitarian societies.[62]

Lastly we may note two variables important in a consideration of the culture structure of individual actors – consistency and complexity. Complexity refers to the number of elements in the individual orientation system and can vary independently for the cognitive, affective and evaluative modes of orientation.[63] Consistency refers to the logical coherence of the individual's orientations. It is naturally difficult to measure these variables in non-experimental research but one can often establish the degree of such complexity and consistency for major historical actors and more generally for different classes and strata. Thus an important factor in the ability to predict and direct the dynamics of social order and dissent in Western bourgeois societies is the knowledge that the periphery has relatively simple and incoherent but acquiescent orientations towards the *status quo*.[64] Likewise marginal intellectuals can often play a major role in social movements through raising the levels of complexity and consistency of peripheral orientation systems.

Culture content and culture structure are thus significant variables in the analysis of social order, reform and revolution. The preference for different combinations of power and rewards affects the radicalism of social movements; their institutionalisation is affected by the relative secularisation of the dominant culture; and the complexity and consistency of orientations affect the ability of a radical movement to adopt successful tactics and strategy in realising its aims. Moreover, the distribution of dissensual and consensual orientations both between centres and throughout society affects fundamentally the possibility of successful mobilisation. It is the combination of structural and cultural perspectives that is required in the development of an adequate understanding of order and change. And in our next chapter we present a symbolic model of societal systems in an attempt to provide the basis of such an understanding.

Summary and Conclusions

In this chapter we have presented an analytical framework for the investigation of social structure and culture in terms of power, exchange and institutionalisation perspectives. We first defined the basic distinction between centre and periphery and then proceeded to a general discussion of the nature of power. The centre comprises those individuals and organisations with power to control the productive processes of different power systems and to determine the distribution of their products. The periphery comprises those excluded from such control and determination. The degree of power hierarchisation (and thus the distinctiveness of centre and periphery) naturally varies across societies and through time. In cultural terms we may distinguish between central and peripheral value systems.

Power is the ability to constrain other actors to do something they would not otherwise do. There are four bases of such power – economic, political, social and cultural. Economic power is based ultimately on control over the means of production, distribution and exchange of goods and services; political power is based ultimately on control over the means of coercion and authorisation; social power is similarly based on control over the means of status attribution; and cultural power is ultimately based on control over the means of value creation and specification. These four types of power are generated in four systems which may or may not be empirically differentiated and controlled by different organisations and individuals.

The power potential of different actors may be used in different types of exchange relations and with variable degrees of reciprocity. The nature of these exchanges reacts back on their power potential and thus determines in large part the dynamics of social order. There are two main types of exchange – that between systems and that within systems. Each power system requires the output of the other three systems if it is to produce its own output in turn. These inputs must be obtained in exchange relations with the other systems. Likewise each system requires both compliance and contributions from members within the system; and these too must be rewarded.

The second major focus in this framework is the cultural system itself. The level of secularisation and the degree of radicalism are the major variables relevant to the analysis of culture content. Secularisation refers to the relative rigidity of normative specifications of value commitments; whereas radicalism refers to the level of social structure or culture to which individuals and organisations are oriented. Among the emergent properties of cultural systems institutional integration and consensus are the most important. The former refers to the consistency of different central value systems; the latter to the average intensity and level of commitment to values throughout society. We argued that both sets of variables are significantly related to the dynamics of social order, reform and revolution.

All that remains now is the presentation of a set of assumptions about exchange, power and institutionalisation so that we can generate our model of order and disorder. The nature of these assumptions should already be apparent from the discussion so far. In our next chapter we make them explicit and present our symbolic model of structural and cultural dynamics.

5 A Theory of Order, Reform and Revolution

We may now turn to the central task of this monograph – the development of a symbolic model of social order, reform and revolution. A symbolic model, it will be recalled, is a theoretical model in which hypotheses are generated by means of conceptual definition and interconnection and by rationally consistent assumptions concerning the nature of the phenomena under investigation. The rationale underlying the present model is derived from power, exchange and institutionalisation perspectives. We have already defined and connected the key concepts in this approach; but an abstract analytical framework is in no sense a theoretical model. Conceptual elaboration and refinement are inadequate unless articulated with a set of mutually consistent and realistic assumptions that permit the generation of testable and meaningful hypotheses. In this chapter we attempt to articulate our analytical framework through the addition of a set of assumptions about the relations between power, exchange, dissent and institutionalisation. Some general propositions about order, reform and revolution are then derived from this combination of concept and assumption. Later developments in the model will undoubtedly need to refine and qualify both assumptions and propositions and we shall suggest further lines of advance in our concluding chapter.

A Set of Assumptions

Three general assumptions underly the whole of the present model of social order. Firstly, we assume that all actors desire some positive combination of different types of power and reward; secondly, we assume that all actors experience deprivation when a disjunction occurs between their 'legitimate'[1] expectations of power and rewards and the gratification of these expectations; and, thirdly, we assume that all actors seek to remove the perceived causes of their deprivation. These three assumptions provide the key to the dynamics of social movements as well as

81

social order; but they must clearly be further specified if they are to be useful in generating relatively determinate propositions.

We therefore suggest that the combination of power and reward desired by actors varies strongly with their location in the power-exchange matrix. More specifically, we assume that the greater the centrality of an actor, the greater his desire for power relative to rewards. This is not an unrealistic assumption and can be justified on both theoretical and empirical grounds (see below). We shall assume that the stronger a given centre, the greater is the desire for that centre's power and rewards. This too is quite a realistic assumption.

Our assumption that the centre is primarily oriented to power and the periphery is primarily oriented to rewards has a number of implications that need to be made explicit. Firstly, in so far as centrality is dependent on organisational factors as well as basic resources, then centrally located actors will attempt to increase their organisational strength and autonomy and will thereby generate conflict among different organisations and systems. Secondly, the periphery's primary orientation towards rewards suggest the potential emergence of commitments to those individuals, organisations or systems able to supply desired rewards. The emergence of such commitments will not only restrict the free flow of peripheral contributions to different productive uses but it will also facilitate the mobilisation of resources through the mediation of economic, political, social or cultural centres. Thirdly, we may note that power incongruence creates a problem in the application of our assumptions to the extent that the power-incongruent combine both central and peripheral locations. In such cases we assume that power orientations always have primacy over reward orientations and thus that the power-incongruent will attempt to equilibrate their position through increasing their power in those systems in which they are less powerful. Fourthly, we may note an apparent falsification of our assumption in the power orientation of the periphery during radical revolutionary periods. Our assumptions imply that this must be due to a blocking of rewards through the operation of the power system; and also that in the post-revolutionary period there will be a de-escalation of desires and demands as new centres crystallise. There is considerable evidence for these implications[2] and we shall therefore retain the assumptions in their present form for the purposes of this model. Finally, we suggest that the differential orientations of centre and periphery are reflected in the orientations of strong and weak centres – with the latter being relatively less oriented to power and thus tending to accommodative rather than autonomous policies.

There is also sound theoretical and empirical justification[3] for the following more specific assumptions about the intensity of deprivation. We assume that the intensity of deprivation varies directly with the extent of the shortfall between expectation and gratification, with the scope or range of the shortfall, and with the salience of the expectations and gratifications involved. We also assume a curvilinear relationship between the intensity of a deprivation and its duration – a relationship manifested in an eventual lowering of expectations and a decrease in the significance of the deprivation. In this connection it is important to note that deprivation is defined in terms of expectations as well as gratification and that control over actors' expectations can thus be employed to lower or to raise the intensity of deprivation independently of the actual level of gratification.[4]

We consider the response to deprivation in more detail in a later section and simply note here that actors may seek to remove the perceived causes of their deprivation individually and/or collectively and that their methods and radicalism may vary considerably. Among the methods available to the centres is the derogation or proscription of actions held to be the cause of central deprivation. Such non-institutionalisation will be backed by more or less severe sanctions to re-establish compliance with central wishes. Institutionalisation is thus related not only to the radicalism and methods of dissensual movements but also with the perceptions and responses to deprivation of the centre.

Before turning to the discussion of responses to deprivation we must first examine the social sources of deprivation and in particular the nature of the conflicts and contradictions within and between power systems that we have but mentioned *en passant* above.

Conflict and Contradiction

There are an infinite number of latent conflicts of interest in every society and it is these that provide the general sources of deprivation in all societies. But it is inherent or emergent contradictions that provide the major sources of the most significant and widespread deprivation, dissent and disorder; and not the myriad non-antagonistic conflicts and personal misfortunes that beset individual actors. There are four main types of contradiction relevant in this context.

The first is inherent in the nature of power itself and concerns the relations of production in a power system. This is the contradiction between the interests of centre and periphery in the distribution of control over the ultimate bases of economic, political, social or cultural power. It is a contradiction that will remain latent, however, as long as the expected differential flow of power and rewards to centre and periphery is maintained. There is a second, parallel, contradiction in the relations among different power systems. This focuses on the contradiction between different centres over domination of their various exchanges and the creation of a surplus for reinvestment or consumption. Owing to the primacy of power orientations among the centres this contradiction is typically manifest rather than latent wherever a differentiated centre exists.

Thirdly, there can be contradictions between the forces and relations of production in any power system. Such a contradiction is not inherent in the nature of power but is contingent on the dynamics of power systems. It emerges when the development of the forces of production creates a potential redistribution of power and/or a potential increase in productivity – realisation of which is inhibited by the extant relations of production. If such contradictions involve deprivation they will intensify the inherent contradictions in the power system and thus lead to more radical conflict. There are similar emergent contradictions in the relations of different power systems. The autonomous development of one's system's forces and relations of production may come into conflict with the developmental tendencies of another system and thus intensify the inherent conflicts between them.

These contradictions clearly vary in their implications for dissent and disorder. The inherent contradictions in a power system can be resolved, on our assumptions, by an appropriate distribution of rewards and adequate control over actors' expectations and over the emergence of power incongruency. The inherent contradiction between power systems, on the other hand, unless the centre is monolithic or power incongruency enforces an accommodative policy on all centres, is conducive to the emergence of radical conflict and disorder. The two emergent contradictions are the most difficult to resolve without radical transformation of society. Where a contradiction between the forces and relations of production is associated with a change in the power potential of different classes or strata, the ability of an isolated centre to control radical dissent will be undermined and a revolutionary transformation of the relations of production is almost an inevitable consequence. The superimposition of such an emergent contradiction on other contradictions, inherent or emergent, in different power systems is obviously even more conducive to radical innovation. Similar considerations apply to the emergent contradictions between power centres and to their combination with contradictions and conflicts in other systems.

These four types of structural contradiction are typically reflected in dissensus, institutional malintegration and 'ideological' conflict in the cultural system. Other inconsistencies and disagreements in the cultural system may also be exploited in the course of dissent in order to encourage or discourage the mobilisation of different classes and strata. It is thus necessary to examine not only the emergence and combination of conflict and contradiction but also the cultural processes whereby individual actors come to recognise and articulate these conflicts and to attempt to resolve them.[5]

The Dynamics of Dissent

Dissent varies greatly in its radicalism, its methods and its institutionalisation as well as its appeal to different classes and strata. Whatever its precise character, however, dissent is invariably due to some form of actual or anticipated deprivation, that is, to an actual or threatened shortfall between expectations and gratifications.[6] It is non-random, socially structured deprivations that are associated with the most consequential forms of dissent. Such deprivations not only affect meaningful groups but also minimise the role of personal factors in the response to deprivation. The more basic the social causes of deprivation, the less important become personal differences and the more radical becomes the dissent.[7] In our brief analysis of the dynamics of deprivation and dissent we must therefore focus disproportionately on the more fundamental conflicts and contradictions in social structures and neglect the more general and mundane sorts of deprivation that produce so rich a variety of responses and attempts to remove the causes of deprivation.

The dynamics of power and exchange relations determine not

only the changing distribution of gratifications but also affect the level of expectations. Changes in the distribution of control over the cultural system and in the power of the cultural centre are thus critical factors in the genesis of deprivation and dissent. A shift in the relative dominance of economic and political centres over the cultural system with the breakout of war, for example, will affect not only the pattern of expectations and deprivations but also the pattern and targets of dissent. The cultural centre is important not only for its impact on expectations but also for its regulation of the responses to deprivation. Apathy, self-blame and scapegoating are often institutionalised modes of response; and all three are clearly inimical to the development of radical dissent. Here again the distribution of power in the cultural system is crucial. Each centre will attempt to direct blame and scapegoating away from itself towards the periphery and/or other power systems; while the periphery will try to establish its own interpretation of deprivation as correct.

Thus even an exploitative power system in which rewards continually decline may avoid radical dissent provided it controls the cultural system and thereby the expectations and responses of peripheral members of the system. A weakening of its control, on the other hand, will typically be associated with a significant increase in dissent and disorder. The success of such an hegemony is dependent on the flexibility of the cultural system relative to social change : where commitments and expectations are too rigid then deprivation will develop and lead to dissent whenever system performance falls short of institutionalised expectations. The maintenance of social order will then depend on the ability of the centre to direct the dissensual response along harmless channels. In the absence of such ideological hegemony an exploitative power system is critically dependent on coercion to maintain the distribution of power and rewards and there will be a constant threat of renewed disorder.

Even socially structured deprivation has significant consequences only when it leads to the belief that it is possible as well as desirable to remove the causes of such deprivation through more or less radical social change. Failure to perceive the causes of deprivation as socially structured – likely where the deprivations are slight and/or the value system emphasises personal responsibility for misfortune – is thus a significant factor in the maintenance of social order. Scapegoating is the least 'rational' mode of response to deprivations that are seen as socially structured. Although scapegoating may seem the logical response in the light of the prevalent assumptions and commitments of the deprived it is 'irrational' because it does not remove the causes of deprivation. None the less scapegoating can develop into more appropriate modes of response provided that the scapegoats belong to the organisation, institution, market or system that is the cause of deprivation and provided also that failure to alleviate the deprivation leads to an escalation of dissent to the correct levels. Where the scapegoats come from outside the relevant organisation, institution, market or system, then an escalation of dissent will still not remove the causes of deprivation. It should perhaps be emphasised at this point that the sanctioning or replacement of individual actors or groups may in fact be sufficient to remove the deprivation. In such circumstances more radical movements will be both unnecessary and possibly counter-productive.

The level of radicalism that characterises dissent depends on three major factors – the location and orientation of those groups subject to deprivation, the strength and distribution of control over the cultural system and the actual causes of deprivation. We discuss each of these factors below.

The orientation of the periphery to rewards rather than to power encourages it to develop initially non-radical modes of response to deprivation : it will take the power system as given and simply attempt to effect a redistribution of rewards.[8] A failure to achieve such a redistribution may lead to an escalation of dissent where the cultural hegemony of the centre is weak. The centre is oriented primarily to power rather than rewards and it will therefore attempt to change the balance of power in response to deprivation (whether this deprivation involves power or only rewards). Similar considerations apply to marginal centre groups with the additional consideration that the marginal centre has a greater interest than the non-marginal centre in more extensive changes in the balance of power since its very centrality is at stake. Where peripheral and marginal and/or central groups are subject to similar or complementary deprivations the periphery may be drawn into more radical dissent that it is at least initially incapable of developing in isolation.

There are also cultural constraints on the development of a radical mode of response to deprivation. If the cultural system is both effective and controlled by the system in which deprivation is felt, then peripheral dissent may not escalate into radical programmes and/or may be diverted into irrelevant channels of protest and change. If the cultural power system is weak or controlled by another centre desirous of undermining the power of the centre in question or, indeed, owing to power incongruency, it is controlled by the deprived periphery, then escalation is much more likely. In this context the ability of the periphery to determine its own values and commitments is critical to the development of a radical dissent where the centre is relatively monolithic and marginal groups are few in number.

Finally, we may note that dissent is most likely to be radical where the conflicts involved in its causation are antagonistic or contradictory – and particularly where these contradictions are emergent rather than inherent in character. Linked with this is the extent to which it is possible to introduce minor changes in social structure. Opposition to such changes and structural constraints on low-level innovations will often encourage the escalation of dissent. In this respect the degree of secularisation is related to radicalism in a paradoxical manner. Sacred cultures specify their values in a rigid fashion and limit individual freedom of interpretation. Thus a strong and consensual sacred culture will inhibit the emergence of even minor dissent since it involves questioning the basic values of the whole system. Conversely a sacred culture that is weak will encourage the escalation of dissent since all levels of social structure are defined in value terms and there is only limited commitment to the general values.

The choice of method is obviously contingent on both the distribution of control over the different power resources and the normative specification of their legitimate employment in different contexts. A strong centre is able both to employ its strategic resources in promoting redistributions of power and rewards and also to deny these resources to others wishing to employ them against the perceived interests of the strong centre. Other centres also have access to diverse power resources through production and exchange relations and they will use these more or less rationally to maintain and extend their power and rewards. The periphery is typically in a weak position and must rely either on 'strike' action by withdrawing its contributions to the production process and/or on appeal to the centre in terms of dominant values. Its ability to strike successfully depends primarily on the relative indispensability of its contributions and the availability of alternative sources of supply; and on the power of the centre to sanction non-compliance by cutting off the supply of rewards and by invoking other centres in its support. The appeal to the centre in terms of dominant values depends for success on the integrity of the centre's commitment to these values and on its acceptance of both the validity and possibility of conceding to the periphery's demands. Where there is power incongruency a periphery may also be able to use its power in other systems to constrain the operation of the system and thereby effect a redistribution of rewards and perhaps also of power in its own favour.

Where the cultural system is effective, normative restrictions are likely to inhibit the most rational employment of power resources in the promotion of the interests of different groups. Particular modes of response to deprivation will be prescribed or encouraged and others derogated or proscribed in such a way as to reinforce the ability of the stronger centres to dominate the society. More generally any radical dissent is likely to be derogated or proscribed and its proponents sanctioned correspondingly. None the less, the more intense the deprivation of a given group and the more radical its dissent, the more likely it is to engage in uninstitutionalised attempts at implementing social change to resolve its deprivation.

Derogation and proscription are important not only because of the normative factors involved but also because they are typically accompanied by more or less severe sanctions. The sanctions employed depend on the centre that derogates or proscribes the dissent and on its links with other centres through actual identity, institutional integration and systemic interdependence. A lack of institutional integration implies the possibility that a given movement will be derogated by some and approved by other centres and such a situation is conducive to the development of dissent because of the partial legitimation and possibly material support that it provides. Likewise the absence of a monolithic centre or of marked interdependence facilitates the development of dissent by limiting the sanctions available to a given centre. Conversely, a monolithic centre or one that is strongly interdependent with other centres is able to mobilise many different types of sanction against dissent and thus to punish non-compliance and reward conformity with more chance of success.

The reaction to derogation and proscription will obviously depend not only on the type and severity of the sanctions involved but also on the relative strength of commitments to the dissensual movement. It is in this context that control over the cultural

89

system is so important since it can be employed to undermine such commitments and to increase the salience of various central punishments and rewards. Where the other centres can control the preferences of dissenters then severe sanctions will generally enforce compliance. But continued resistance will force the centre either to institutionalise the movement and concede its claims or to attempt its elimination through starvation or coercion. In the latter case a persecuted movement must either withdraw from the society or develop alternative sources of food, other goods and services, military protection and policy benefits, in addition to maintaining control over commitments and deference behaviour. The escalation of dissent and derogation thus leads eventually to a basic force situation in which the outcome depends entirely on the balance of power between the contending forces.

A revolutionary movement must therefore develop alternative bases of power if it is to successfully implement radical social change. These bases may develop autonomously with the emergence of contradictions between the forces and relations of production and between the different power systems. In such circumstances a radical movement has only to realise the potential redistribution of power created by such contradictions. In all other cases the radical movement must deliberately initiate a shift in the balance of power by creating its own power bases *de novo* or by mobilising resources from exogenous sources of supply. As understanding of the revolutionary process is more widely diffused we may expect an increasing reliance on deliberate attempts to shift the balance of power and create autonomous revolutionary economic, political, social and cultural power systems. The success of such 'dual power'[9] strategies depends on the ability to establish all four power bases and on the relevance of the strategy to the particular pattern of contradictions and conflicts in the society. There is no general formula the application of which ensures success.[10]

The dynamics of dissent are thus dependent on several different but interrelated factors. Dissent is conditioned by conflict and contradiction and precipitated by deprivation. The radicalism and methods of dissent depend on the groups subject to deprivation and the nature of the underlying conflicts; on the pattern of control over the cultural system and its general strength and effectiveness; and on the more general distribution of control over different types and levels of resources. The ability of a dissensual movement to appeal to different deprived groups is dependent primarily on the way in which the deprivations can be articulated with the aims of the movement. A radical programme presented in esoteric contexts without mention of the rewards that derive from its implementation and bearing little relation to the phenomenology of deprivation will certainly hold little appeal for the deprived groups at the periphery. A radical programme that emphasises the relation between deprivation and the structure of power, that is effectively communicated in readily understood phrases, that is relevant to the phenomenology of deprivation, and that is presented in the context where deprivation occurs, is likely to hold much greater appeal. And it is the ability to appeal to the maximum number of deprived groups that determines the ability to implement radical change in an orderly and peaceful fashion after a revolution.

The Conditions of Social Order

In the light of these assumptions and the general framework outlined in this and earlier chapters, we can derive the conditions under which social order, i.e., peaceful coexistence in the operation of social institutions, is possible. The absence or negation of these conditions will be associated with disorder.

The first set of conditions under which we find social order is one in which all members of the system have equal power – subject to force activation – and where the output of secondary rewards is optimal. Social order will exist because the inherent contradictions of any power system are attenuated and every actor is able to ensure a fair share of rewards through the exercise of power. Disorder is likely where the dynamics of one or more power systems operate to disrupt the general equality of power and where there are no institutionalised mechanisms to ensure a redistribution or destruction of surplus rewards and resources and thus guarantee continuing equality.

A second type of society in which social order is likely is one in which there is power hierarchisation combined with reciprocity or even benefaction in exchange relations. Under such a system the periphery would have its desire for rewards gratified and the centre would be able to maintain power. Manifestation of the contradictions inherent in any power relation will thus be minimised and dissent is likely to be non-radical and institutionalised. Disorder in such a society is likely to result from technological or other changes that produce exploitation and a

91

cut in the periphery's rewards. More generally the emergence of contradictions between the forces and relations of production may generate deprivation at both centre and periphery and thus lead to more radical and hence less institutionalised dissent.

Lastly there is a third type of society in which social order is possible under the assumptions set out above. This is one in which there is both power hierarchisation and exploitation by the centre but where there is also strong central control over the expectations and commitments of the periphery so that it does not experience deprivation. Instabilities in this type of social order derive from loss of control over the cultural system and/or from manifest system ineffectiveness relative to institutionalised expectations. Both these factors may in turn be due to emergent contradictions or the development of a marginal centre group and they will be further aggravated by the development of dissent.

These three types obviously need further specification and elaboration. In particular one needs to know under what conditions each type of society is likely to develop and persist. The first situation is unlikely except in conditions of limited 'technological' development in each power system with a correspondingly limited 'production' so that the accumulation and investment of primary or secondary resources is difficult. Where such accumulation does occur there must be effective institutionalised mechanisms to ensure the redistribution or destruction of these resources to prevent the disruption of the system through personal aggrandisement. Dissent in such societies is likely to focus on emergent inequalities in power and attempts to increase these inequalities – especially when unaccompanied by benefaction or at least reciprocity – will be strongly derogated. Where power inequalities emerge but are beneficial the system will develop into our second type.

The second type is likely to develop and persist only where there is marked power incongruency. In such a situation the periphery in any given system will be able to prevent exploitation through 'strike' action and by employing its power in other systems to control the centre. Where power incongruency is weakened, however, 'strikes' will be more readily repressed and inequalities and exploitation will emerge. The system will then become dissensual and disorderly unless the emergent strong centre that appears with declining incongruency is able to establish an effective cultural hegemony and transform the system into the third type of society. The latter depends for continuing order

92

on the maintenance of an effective cultural system in which all members of the society are socialised into acceptance of the central values and the dominant distribution of power and rewards. This ideological hegemony may be based on control over the cultural system by another centre or on a strong cultural centre powerful in its own right. It is essential that the institutionalised expectations and commitments be sufficiently flexible to prevent the emergence of deprivation and dissent when the flow of rewards varies; and also for such dissent as does develop to be channelled into harmless, non-radical directions. Such societies will also become unstable where the cultural system is ineffective and marginal centre groups or power incongruency develop. The extent of radical change will then depend on the orientations and on the balance of power of contending groups.

Even in this brief account we have shown that these three different types of society are potentially unstable and disorderly. They can develop into other types of orderly society or into societies with widespread uninstitutionalised dissent. Technological development in the first type of society, for example, can produce emergent inequalities that create disorder or transform society into the second type of social order. Likewise the emergence of power incongruency in the third type of society may initiate a transformation into a beneficial hierarchic society or contribute to the disintegration of the exploitative and inegalitarian system.

The same basic considerations apply to the analysis of disorder and we have already discussed some aspects of the dynamics of uninstitutionalised dissent. We shall now describe the conditions which are most conducive to social disorder.

The first type of society in which disorder will be significant is one in which there is a monolithic centre with limited cultural power confronted by a totally exploited periphery. In such a society dissent will initially be non-radical in character since the periphery lacks the means to develop a more radical critique of the power structure. The dynamics of proscription and repression should, however, generate more radical dissent and the emergence of more intense deprivation. But unless the periphery can develop a 'dual power' system its dissent is most unlikely to lead to the successful implementation of radical changes. As proscription and repression continue, the deprivations may become less intense and the low level of gratification accepted as normal. This will result in a pragmatic acquiescence in the system until gratifications decline again and dissent will thus repeat a cyclical pattern of intermittent and more or less radical protest followed by greater or lesser periods of passivity. Only with the development of power incongruency within this society or the emergence of contradictions between forces and relations of production in the different power systems will this cyclical pattern be altered and more radical changes be capable of realisation.

While such a monolithic and exploitative centre is particularly prone to intermittent dissent and disorder, another type of society is likely to be characterised by more continuous and radical dissent. This is a society in which there is a differentiated centre and where one of the centres is subject to emergent contradictions between the forces and relations of production. Within the latter system the centre and periphery will both try to maintain their previous level of rewards – the centre by increasing exploitation, the periphery by reducing exploitation. Marginal groups are also likely to develop at the centre of such a system and to articulate radical dissent which may appeal to the periphery, the non-marginal centre or to other centres for support. The other centres will also attempt to maintain their 'market share' of the contradictory system's product in order to maintain their own levels of production. The other centres will thus come into conflict with each other as well as with the ailing centre and its periphery. Failure to maintain this 'market share' will mean a reduction in the output of other centres and thus lead to deprivation and dissent among their peripheries. Deflationary processes are likely to result in all systems as their centres and peripheries resort to more basic sanctions to maintain their share of power and rewards in the face of declining outputs. The outcome of these conflicts will depend on the balance of power between different groups and on the different alliances that may be made. The result may vary from the disintegration of the whole society to the emergence of a stronge centre able to dominate the other centres and their peripheries. In the latter case the nature and stability of the regime that results will depend on the type of strong centre that develops and on the orientations of the other members of society.

These two types of disorderly society are similar in various respects to the second and third types of orderly society that we discussed above. The major difference between the revolutionary system based on a monolithic and exploitative centre and that in which the exploitative system is orderly is simply the presence or absence of ideological hegemony (or 'value consensus'). While the major difference between the orderly pluralistic and beneficial system and the disorderly pluralistic society is the presence in the latter of emergent contradictions between the various forces and relations of production. These similarities should serve to emphasise the basic instabilities of orderly societies and their potential transformation into less orderly, more revolutionary systems.

So far in our discussion we have neglected explicit mention of the role of inflation in the genesis of deprivation and dissent. The essence of inflation is that it combines a rise in effective demand for various resources or rewards with an inability on the part of potential suppliers to provide these resources and rewards. This contradiction may be due to an autonomous expansion of demand followed by responsive increases in rates of exchange; and/or to aggressive increases in exchange rates followed by an expansion in effective demand that results either from the attempts of one or more centres to counter the potential deflationary effects of such increases and/or from the effects of the increased rewards to those who have successfully raised their incomes.[11] Inflation can occur both within power systems and between power systems. Whatever its cause and whatever its location, however, it results in deprivation for at least some members of the society and thus leads to dissent of one kind or another. Inflationary processes need not be confined to complex, differentiated societies in which there is a marked development of generalised media of exchange. They can also occur in relatively simple societies. An increase in the material wealth of the Kwakiutl Indians, for example, has been linked to the 'potlatch' phenomenon in which material wealth is destroyed in competition for prestige and political power.[12]

Uninstitutionalised dissent can also occur in many other types of society, including those mainly characterised by social order. The structures and processes underlying deprivation and dissent have been described in earlier sections and they can appear even in otherwise orderly societies and thereby contribute to their disruption and transformation. Instability in social order should not, however, be confused with instability in the basic structures of society. The extent to which disorder is accompanied by structural change is dependent on many factors ranging from the degree of radicalism of social movements and the conduciveness of the wider society, to the balance of power between contending forces and the response of the different centres. Moreover, fundamental changes can be implemented in an institutionalised manner (particularly in beneficial or reciprocal hierarchic societies) and thus take the form of reform rather than revolution. In describing the conditions and limits of social order we are also describing the conditions and limits of reform.

This analysis can also be linked to our interest in social justice. Not all the sets of conditions conducive to social order are also conducive to social justice. The first and second types of orderly society are clearly those most closely linked to the realisation of social justice. In the first type of society inequalities are limited and emergent inequalities are approved only when they lead to general benefits; the equality of power also contributes to the maximisation of individual liberty of action subject to others having a like liberty. However, the limited technological development and the importance of consensus in such societies limit the potential scope of liberties and range of action. The second type of society is also conducive to justice. Inequalities are again dependent on services rendered rather than on exploitation; while liberties can be more extensive in scope owing to the greater differentiation and freedom of action this implies. However, this system is more unstable than the first and the essential factor of power incongruency could be held to conflict with the institutionalisation of equal opportunities of access to all positions of power. None the less both types of society are unmistakably more just than the third type of orderly society in which inequality and exploitation are maintained by ideological hegemony and false consciousness; and in which social movements to attain justice are derogated and repressed. The transformation of such a society into a less exploitative and inegalitarian system is dependent not only on the emergence of contradictions that undermine the ability of the centre(s) to defend their position but also on the emergence and successful proselytisation of movements oriented to social justice. Unfortunately this latter requirement may not always coincide with the emergence of the former contradictions.

Conclusions

In this chapter we have presented the main outlines of a symbolic model of social order, reform and revolution. It is clear that this is not a fully developed theory and it is not intended as such. Rather we have attempted to show how the combination of different contemporary approaches to structural analysis can contribute to a deeper and more complex understanding of the

96

dynamics of order, reform and revolution in all societies. More specifically we have been concerned in this chapter with the articulation of the basic analytical framework outlined in earlier pages. To this end we presented a set of assumptions and then showed how they can be employed to derive some very general propositions about the nature of order and disorder. In the following pages we attempt to put some 'flesh' on these different models and processes through the presentation of a number of specific case studies. We shall also provide a more detailed specification of the conditions of order and stability in differentiated societies with various types of strong centre.

6 Studies in Order, Reform and Revolution – I

In this and the next chapter we expand on the conditions of social order and disorder outlined in the preceding pages. In illustrating and amplifying these earlier remarks we will draw on various case studies of order, reform and revolution and relate them to our general model of social structure. We begin with an analysis of relatively undifferentiated and egalitarian societies and later examine more differentiated and inegalitarian systems.

Simple Societies

Our first set of conditions for social order was found in a society in which power was distributed more or less equally, subject to force activation, and the production of secondary resources was optimal at the current level of economic, political, social and cultural technology. This set of conditions is most obviously realised in 'simple societies', that is, relatively undifferentiated societies with simple technologies. There are two basic types of such simple societies that meet these conditions – the primitive band and the classical segmentary lineage society. In bands we find that nearly all social relations are mediated by kinship; kinship is also important in segmentary lineage societies but these also have more complex types of relation. In both types of society, however, power is distributed more or less equally and productivity in the various power systems is optimal but limited. Thus economic and political outputs are comparatively low owing to the limited technologies of production and destruction; while the social and cultural power systems are more productive and social power is relatively inegalitarian. Such inequalities as do exist are generally based on contributions to the common good or are dependent on benefaction for stability.

The *primitive band* has a very simple structure. The band is small, unspecialised and nomadic within a given territorial area. The only division of labour is based on age and sex differentiation. There is only limited technological development and there can be no economic surplus for investment or exploitation within the economic system – goods must either be consumed or exchanged for non-economic rewards and resources. Military technology is also simple and every adult male can provide more or less the same equipment and skills. These two factors preclude any marked inegalitarian distribution of economic or political power and rewards. While elder males and shamans tend to have more prestige and influence they must none the less work and they lack situational sanctions with which to support their power base. Their influence is dependent on benefaction or reciprocity and exploitation is sanctioned by loss of prestige.

Although the band society is basically egalitarian and production is optimal there are still inevitable conflicts and contradictions over the distribution of power and rewards. These conflicts focus on *emergent* inequalities and imbalances in different exchanges. They are typically controlled by institutionalised mechanisms that enforce the redistribution of rewards and generalised reciprocity in all social relations. Continuing conflict is met by a resort to self-help or self-protection, to social ostracism and shaming, and to fission of the band. Such reactions to conflict and dissent are possible because of the basic equality of power and the general commitment to the patterns of reciprocal exchange. It is only with the emergence of contradictions between the various forces and relations of production that the primitive band becomes less orderly and stable. These contradictions emerge only with difficulty, however, and the relative persistence of the band form of organisation during human evolution is sure testimony to this.[1]

The main internal contradiction that emerges to disrupt the primitive band form of social organisation is rooted in the technological and demographic base of the band. The development of simple horticulture or of a maritime or pastoral economy encourages at least semi-permanent sedentary communities and the growth of population. The combination of these factors in turn probably encourages the segmentation of the band within a localised setting. The band is thus transformed into a segmentary lineage society. External factors may also precipitate the transformation of the band and its incorporation into more complex societal systems or indeed its complete disintegration.

The *classical segmentary lineage society* is based on interconnections between a number of different lineages. A lineage is a corporate group of unilineal kin with a formalised system of authority and with defined rights and duties in its corporate

99

capacity. It is generally named and there is an accepted genea-logical relationship between all its members. A lineage may be subdivided or segmented into smaller groupings, each with genealogies of smaller depth and narrower span. While lineages are clearly found in many types of society it is the dominant role of the segmentary lineage that defines this particular type and distinguishes it relative to others.

In the classical segmentary lineage society nearly all relations are mediated by kinship connections. In the economy, for example, access to land, to livestock, to women and to other facilities is vested in the lineage; likewise authority in the political system is defined in kinship terms and lineages provide the basic unit for feuding, blood-compensation payments or exactions, warfare and self-help. Within the stratification system status is based largely on position within the lineage system – though achievement is an important secondary base of prestige. The lineage is also the basis of socialisation and religious commitment.

In such societies the lineages are arranged hierarchically and each level is significant in different circumstances and in con-nection with different types of resources and rewards. While each level has comparable and hence conflicting interests the competi-tion at one level is balanced by complementary interests at a higher level. Each lineage is also typically able to match the power of another lineage of comparable depth and width and this basic equality also contributes to the stability of the society. Emergent contradictions can often be handled by a simple redefinition or realignment of the lineages and their segments. Thus the interlocking or nesting of segments and the possibility of reorganisation ensure the basic continuity and stability of the overall society without need for a unifying single power centre.[2]

As in primitive bands there is room for conflict over the dis-tribution of secondary resources and rewards in such segmentary lineage societies; but there is also considerably more scope for conflict over the distribution of control over the ultimate bases of power. The emergence of marked inequalities and continuous open conflict are none the less inhibited by the system of com-plementary opposition, by the basic equality of power (especially between equivalent lineages), and by the still limited degree of technological development. These three factors are reinforced by a variety of structural constraints and institutionalised mechanisms of conflict resolution. Thus the exogamy rule enforces the main-tenance of friendly relations with potentially opposed lineages

100

owing to the need to exchange women and also to the cross-cutting ties that are created by intermarriage. Self-help and self-protection through political sanctions (e.g. feuding) and through ritual sanctions (e.g. witchcraft and sorcery accusations) are further institutionalised modes of social conflict. There are also institutionalised equivalents to feuding (e.g. blood-compensation) and institutionalised arbitrators who have both political and ritual sanctions to enforce their decisions. Failure to resolve a conflict by these and other legitimate means can lead eventually to fission between the conflicting segments. The very fact that this process of segmentation is both structurally possible and normatively permissible means that more radical dissent is less likely than where attempts at resolving conflicts through low-level changes are impossible or blocked by the centre. In this way the basic structure of the society remains stable and relations between different groups are conducted in a more or less orderly fashion.[3]

The classical segmentary lineage society is found less often than segmentary lineage societies with additional and secondary bases of association. In many segmentary lineage societies there have developed forms of organisation or association which are not based on kinship, for example, secret societies, earth cults, age-regiments, age grades and village councils.[4] These developments will obviously affect the basic conflicts and contradictions found in segmentary societies and thus affect also their potentialities for orderly or revolutionary change.

Segmentary lineage societies tend to remain stable owing to their structure of cross-cutting and complementary oppositions and their fundamental consensus on the basic values and institutions. But they can also break down or change under certain circumstances. Their transformation may be due to the emergence of internal contradictions or to the impact of external forces such as trade or conquest or culture contact. The main internal contradictions include the emergence of differential productivity or occupational specialisation between lineages; the development of client lineages attached to other lineages following the segmentation of the attached lineage from another; the impact of demographic changes on productivity and the exchange of women; and the development of different military technologies. One of the most important effects of such contradictions is a decline in the general equivalence of lineages in marital exchange, political and economic power, ritual status, and so forth. While

101

the emergence of such inequalities is compatible with continuing social order if combined with reciprocity or benefaction (or effective cultural or ritual constraints), it will lead to dissent and disorder if combined with exploitation and weak cultural constraints. In the latter case segmentation or fission of the less powerful lineages may follow provided that there is limited interdependence, limited military inequality and the possibility of geographical mobility.

These points are illustrated in the *gumsa-gumlao* cycle found among the Kachin Hills people of Highland Burma. The *gumlao* system ideally comprises a cluster or several clusters of highland villages in which the lineages are equal in power and in rights. These lineages are exogamous and women are exchanged in a circle based on matrilateral cross-cousin marriage. Within the lineage siblings all have equal status and there is a continual process of segmentation or fission. Within the village lineages all have equal title to the land provided they are among the original founders of the village; while judicial authority is vested in a Council of Elders drawn from the localised lineage segments resident in the village. Although this system is ideally egalitarian and republican in structure, however, it is difficult to maintain the theoretical equality of status between lineages. Particular village headmen and lineages become increasingly dominant and attempt to establish an inegalitarian, aristocratic system modelled on the lowland Shan society. The Kachin version of this hierarchical and potentially exploitative system is found in the *gumsa* ideal. This prescribes the internal stratification of the village clusters on the basis of lineage rank and the economic, political and ritual dominance of the royal or chiefly lineage.

This dominant position is manifested in the royal lineage's monopoly of land, in tribute, in marriage payments that vary directly with the rank of the bridegroom, in compensation payments that vary directly with the rank of the victim, in ritual virtues hereditary in the royal lineage, and so forth. The marriage system in such a society is hypogamous – women marry into a lineage of the same or lower rank, men marry into a lineage of the same or higher rank as their own. The men of a chiefly lineage always marry women from similar lineages in other chiefly domains. Succession is based on ultimogeniture in combination with seniority of the mother if the household is polygamous. Lineage segmentation is fairly frequent and the resulting segments are ranked according to the relative status of the siblings involved.

There is clearly a considerable difference between these two ideals – but it is rarely realised in practice and most communities display features of both. Moreover, just as the *gumlao* system tends to break down and develop lineage stratification, the *gumsa* system likewise tends to break down and develop egalitarian and republican features. The *gumlao* system is unstable when the headmen (or others) have access to economic wealth due to the development of cash crops, to strategic positions on trade routes, or to the possibility of exploiting lowland wet-rice cultivators. This wealth is used to validate claims to aristocratic or chiefly status through ostentatious ritual and benefaction. Provided the emergent royal lineage is beneficial or reciprocative in its relations with other lineages, it remains unchallenged although subordinate chiefly lineage segments may establish new settlements elsewhere. But the attempt of the royal lineage to repudiate the obligations of affinal and cognatic kinship and to rely on bond-slaves for political and economic support will typically precipitate opposition from both the inferior lineages and the subordinate chiefly lineage segments. The opposition usually attempts to depose the chiefly lineage or restrict its power in the name of *gumlao* principles and is often led by the chief's elder brother(s) whose position is particularly threatened by a repudiation of cognatic obligations. Failure to depose the dominant lineage segment may be followed by fission and the establishment of a new settlement based either on *gumlao* principles or the leadership of the elder brother's lineage segment. In either case the stage is set for a renewed oscillation between the two ideals.[5]

Such an oscillatory pattern is certainly not typical of all segmentary lineage societies and is dependent on several particular structural and ecological circumstances. It none the less illustrates the main principles involved in the dynamics of social order and dissent in such societies. The egalitarian *gumlao* system tends to change in a more or less orderly fashion as long as the emergent inequalities are associated with reciprocity and beneficence in terms of Kachin concepts and values. The *gumlao* system itself is also orderly and associated with rapid segmentation and fission in the manner of more typical segmentary lineage societies. Finally the *gumsa* system becomes disorderly and unstable when it becomes exploitative and the chiefly centre attempts to transform the society into a Shan system based on caste distinctions and slavery rather than lineage co-operation and reciprocity.

Thus the simple society in the main exemplifies the charac-

103

teristics of our first type of orderly society. The maintenance of order depends on the combination of egalitarian power and generalised reciprocity with a basic commitment to the cultural system and structural constraints on the emergence of inequalities and exploitation. There are obviously still conflicts between actors and lineages and these are expressed in myth and ritual as well as in everyday behaviour. But most conflicts are institutionalised and lead to minor reforms in social structure (e.g. segmentation and fission) rather than to revolutionary transformations of the system. It is the emergence of additional contradictions that initiates more radical changes in social structure and even these may be accompanied by continuing order provided the change is compatible with continuing reciprocity or benefaction. The potentialities of order in societies with emergent inequalities have already been discussed above in connection with the *gumsa* system and we now turn to a more detailed analysis in the next section.

Inequality and Reciprocity

The second type of society in which we argued there would be social order is one in which there is power hierarchisation combined with reciprocity or benefaction in the different power systems. The maintenance of reciprocity or benefaction depends primarily on the maintenance of power incongruency between the different power systems. The range of such societies is wider than for the preceding type although they are rarely found in as pure a form; and the relative importance of different power centres varies somewhat. These systems are also less stable and more prone to disorder than the simple egalitarian society owing to tendencies for power incongruency to break down and lead to exploitation and deprivation. Our illustrations are drawn primarily from the still relatively simple African chiefdoms and kingdoms and from the impact of changes in these societies.

The structure of the historical African states varies considerably but it is none the less limited in most cases by two major factors – their stationary subsistence economies and their limited military technologies.[6] The economic system necessitated the widespread dispersal of the population while the limited productivity combined with typically limited trade and material luxuries to inhibit the establishment of an exploitative economic centre. But the emergence in some states of commodity trade, slave

104

trading and occupational specialisation encouraged such developments and had a corresponding impact on the dynamics of dissent. Secondly, since all men could supply their own weapons and the level of military technology was low, an exploitative military or political centre was also difficult to establish. But the emergence of more advanced military organisation (e.g. the Zulu regimental system) and the introduction of cavalry and the gun obviously encouraged the militarisation and centralisation of society. None the less these two limiting factors were generally effective in preventing exploitative domination and in facilitating decentralisation and local autonomy. Moreover, while local leaders represented the chief or king, they were also dependent on local support for the maintenance of their power and thus localised exploitation was also inhibited.

Within these broad limits there was considerable variation in the precise structure of power and particularly in the degree of power incongruency. Power incongruency is obviously a variable phenomenon and its potential clearly depends on the level of differentiation in the society. In relatively undifferentiated societies in which many rewards and resources are still embedded in ascriptive territorial groups or kinship groups and cultural technology is primitive, the sheer inability of an emergent power centre to control other power systems is an important constraint on congruency. In more differentiated societies one would also need indications that the periphery in one system was actively powerful in another to assert the presence of congruency. There is clearly considerable incongruency in this weaker sense in the African kingdoms and chiefdoms. Local and kinship groups are important in the distribution of power, resources and rewards; and there is necessarily considerable administrative and military decentralisation. The cultural power system is relatively diffuse and there are strong traditional constraints on the exercise of power. Moreover, peripheral members of lineages and local groups were represented at the centre through lineage heads and elders and through local chiefs or headmen whose power was dependent on their continuing support. The development of clientship in such societies had similar effects. Lastly in many of these societies we also find institutionalised incongruencies – ranging from the bicentralisation of power between chief and secret societies in certain West African systems to the division of military, political and ritual functions between several dominant lineages in other African polities.[7]

105

The structure of power in such societies was thus generally conducive to reciprocity and social order. Within the lineage or local group we find many of the same conflicts and institutionalised modes of resolution as in segmentary lineage societies. But we also find conflicts and contradictions in the distribution of centralised power. In particular the cultural system and the distribution of power were favourable to the emergence of movements to replace the king or chief. The ambiguity of succession rules combined with the administrative and military decentralisation to create numerous legitimate and potential claimants for the throne. The traditional legitimation of the ruler stressed his generosity and his connection with the fertility and prosperity of the land. Thus exploitation or injustice, crop or cattle failure, military disaster, or even the ruler's ill-health, could precipitate movements to replace the king or chief. Although only members of the royal line(s) could accede to the throne there was ample scope for commoner chiefs to seek power through supporting one of the claimants or the incumbent. More peripheral members would support the claimant or local chief who provided most benefits and they could not be punished for their support of a rebel. Unsuccessful rebellion was followed by the death or flight of the claimant. An alternative to such a movement was the attempt to establish independent chiefdoms on the fringes of the main state or to migrate and establish an autonomous state elsewhere. Cycles of rebellion or fission were more or less institutionalised in these societies and served *in part* to limit the exploitativeness of the centralised power and to facilitate the continuity and stability of the basic structures of power. But the limited interdependence associated with this type of power incongruency encouraged the development of secessionist movements as well as movements to replace central authorities. Thus we find a longer term oscillation between rebellion within a large state and fragmentation into a number of smaller states.[8]

The development of widespread trade and/or more sophisticated military organisation and techniques necessarily created emergent contradictions between the forces and relations within and between the different power systems. These contradictions were resolved in more centralised and powerful centres with economic hierarchisation and interdependence as well as with specialised administrative and military staffs. With the decline in power incongruency relative to the less centralised states there developed increasing exploitation – although if centralisation coincided with increasing productivity the actual level of rewards for the periphery may not have declined.[9] Continuing differentiation and urbanisation produced even more marked inequalities and exploitation and were associated with distinct changes in the patterns of deprivation and dissent. Thus the ties between the horticultural classes and local leaders became attenuated and localised rebellions were less frequent; moreover, the increased interdependence made secession more difficult and more severely sanctioned. While localised rebellion for the throne and for secession declined in significance there was an increased potential for peasant revolt against the urbanised centre. At the same time the city-mob and the soldiery became increasingly important potential sources of support in the struggle for power at the centre. Succession rules were also tightened so that legitimate rivals were fewer in number and there was a corresponding rise in struggles for power in the royal household rather than for the kingship itself. There was thus a general tendency to move towards a society with intermittent and more or less radical disorder based on a monolithic and exploitative centre and away from a society based on inequality and reciprocity.[10]

It would clearly be a significant and useful test of our model to relate variations in power incongruency in these societies to levels of exploitation and disorder. Unfortunately the present writer lacks a sufficient command over the materials and much of the required data is missing. But there does seem to be general support for the implications of our model. The most orderly societies would seem to be those where the chief has very limited power or, indeed, a ritual and symbolic position only (e.g. the divine kingship of the Shilluk). In such emergent 'segmentary states' there was considerable decentralisation and both fission and rebellion were institutionalised.[11] Likewise those 'bicentralised' polities (e.g. the Kpelle of Liberia) in which there is an equipendency between king and secret societies also appear to have been particularly orderly. Conversely, those in which the king came to dominate the societies became more inegalitarian and more prone to disorder.[12] Disorder was still more likely with the development of centralisation, greater inequality and an emergent military stratum; but the continuing importance of the traditional 'redistributive ethic'[13] and the limited nature of the cultural centre restrained the levels of exploitation. The establishment of conquest societies unaccompanied by the incorporation of the conquered tribes or lineages was yet more conducive

107

to the pattern of intermittent and more or less radical dissent that we have described above. This pattern was attenuated only where the cultural power of the centre was greatly increased – thus the Zulu kingdom under Shaka allegedly developed a system of terroristic despotism that combined the twin features of our third type of orderly society, that is, exploitation and hegemony.[14]

It was from similar patrimonial or conquest societies (as well as from more developed feudal systems) that the historical bureaucratic empires generally developed.[15] The development of such empires was associated with a shift towards the increasing exploitation of the periphery and a corresponding pattern of intermittent and more or less radical dissent. But it was not incompatible with the presence at lower levels of social organisation of communities characterised primarily by inequality, reciprocity and social order. The Indian village community and its more inclusive regional community provide an interesting albeit impure and partial illustration.

The village community existed in comparative isolation from the superordinate state system. It was based primarily on socio-cultural power exercised through the extended family and the pervasive caste system and was reinforced by the distribution of control over land. Political power was largely important for its exactions rather than for its protection and policy benefits. The political centres were also typically less continuous, less strong and less legitimate than in other historical empires owing to their lack of a stable reference point in local values and structures. Increasing political exploitation and/or weakening of the state system owing to the intensification of internal contradictions typically led, therefore, to the village communities seeking independence from superordinate power rather than to replace one set of imperial rulers with another. These secessionist rebellions were a major element in the pattern of intermittent disorder in such inegalitarian and exploitative societies. They were generally led by, and focused on, local landlords who had established a measure of independence and who were comparatively beneficial in exercising their power. Since land was generally plentiful prior to British rule there were incentives for peasant cultivators to move off to less exploitative landlords and for landlords to be relatively lenient in their exactions. Thus as Mogul power became more repressive and corrupt such secessionist movements became more frequent; but they still did not assume the significance of

108

peasant movements in empires where the local community was also exploitative.[16]

At the local level the caste system was extremely varied and he would be a rash person who would argue that the system was always beneficial or even reciprocative in character.[17] Within each main linguistic region there were over 200 major castes and some 2000 minor caste groups or *jati*. The latter are small hereditary and endogamous groups practising a traditional occupation and enjoying a measure of economic, juridical, social and cultural autonomy within limits set by a rigid hierarchy of ritual prestige or status. The rigidity of the division of labour and the pervasiveness of the caste mode of organisation ensured a generally marked interdependence between the different castes which were thereby ordered into a closed but organic system of power and exchange relations. This interdependence with its associated rights and duties limited exploitation and provided all but the most peripheral members (such as drummers and sweepers) with a niche in society. Moreover, since high castes were often more numerous than lower castes and land was not generally scarce, the former often had to compete for the services of cultivators and artisans and this placed further limits on the exploitativeness of the locally powerful castes.[18] However, the general congruency of economic, social and cultural power was not conducive to the maintenance of reciprocity and there were thus constant tendencies towards increasing exploitation. Thus the growth of the peasant population and the concomitant pressure on land combined with the extension of rural capitalism and the money market to increase the exploitativeness of landlords under both the East India Company and direct British governmental rule. This pattern was particularly marked where the British established proprietary rights in land themselves and on behalf of those responsible for the payment of land revenue to the state and in place of the customary rights of cultivators and/or village control over its distribution and cultivation.[19] In such circumstances the peasantry was prone to intermittent dissent especially where there was a polarisation between landlord and cultivator rather than a pattern of sub-letting and rack-renting with proprietors also labouring for others.[20]

While economic exploitation at the local level was thus often limited prior to British rule, the status hierarchisation and segregation of the caste system was both arbitrary and exploitative in character. The caste hierarchy was determined with reference to the life-style and values of the dominant caste and was at least theoretically permanently ordered. But collective mobility was actually both possible and common especially among castes whose secular (economic and political) power was incongruent with their ritual (social and cultural) power. Such mobility could be achieved through the adoption of less polluting life-styles and by acceptance of Brahminic or other dominant caste values. This process of upward mobility through Sanskritisation was generally opposed by the other caste groups and was a major focus of conflicts and contradiction within the system. Its success depended on the acknowledgement of the new status by other castes and especially on that of the dominant caste.[21] Individual mobility was also possible through a life of prayer and asceticism. The caste system was so firmly institutionalised that even low castes complained not about the system as a whole but their location within it; and so pervasive that even dissensual movements were incorporated into the system itself as subcastes – ranging from criminal or bandit castes such as the Thuggees to radical religious movements such as Jainists, Buddhists, Lingayats or Christians. In more recent times caste has shown its adaptability through its urban and political manifestations.[22] Indeed so firmly institutionalised and pervasive has been the caste system that a good case could be made, especially after the imposition of British rule, for including it under our third type of orderly society, that is, one combining exploitation with hegemony.

Cultural power as well as social power was exercised largely by the Brahmin castes and this was particularly true where Brahmins either owned land or had assured revenues from other castes. Their hegemony was tempered by constraints on the degree of economic and political exploitation possible due to the technological, ecological and structural conditions prior to British rule; and it is for this reason that we have considered the village community as an impure but interesting illustration of an inegalitarian and reciprocative society. In return for the peripheral contributions to the economic, social and cultural systems, the dominant castes provided cleared land, economic management, juridical services in village councils, acknowledgement of ritual status contingent on fulfilling one's caste duties and on Sanskritisation, rationalisations for low status, ritual services, and so forth.[23] The level of exploitation obviously varied through time and across communities and the caste system is both arbitrary and unjust according to our criteria; but there is some support in

110

the literature for the view that definite positive services were provided and that dissent took relatively institutionalised forms. It was in the more despotic relations between imperial powers and local communities and in the later developments and exploitation under colonial domination that dissent became more violent and disorderly.

Thus in both African polities and Indian village communities there were tendencies towards reciprocity or benefaction in the relations between the more and the less powerful. In turn these tendencies were associated with relatively non-radical and institutionalised dissent. Where more exploitative tendencies developed (and, as we have stressed, they were never entirely absent) there was a more marked reaction whose success depended on the balance of power. Generally speaking, the power incongruencies of the Indian system favoured the dominant castes whereas the distribution of power in most African chiefdoms favoured a return to a more reciprocative pattern. In both cases it would clearly be useful to investigate the more detailed implications of our model in the light of variations in the degree of power congruency, exploitativeness and dissent. Further investigation is certainly required before we can say that these illustrations in any sense validate our model. But we must now turn to focus more directly on those societies and situations in which inequality is combined with exploitation rather than reciprocity or benefaction. Case studies from such societies are presented in the next chapter.

Conclusions

In this chapter we have presented case studies drawn largely from simple African and Asian societies to illustrate two types of society favourable to social order. In describing these as orderly we do not mean to imply that they are without conflict and social change; but only that the conflict and change typical of such societies is non-radical and institutionalised. It should also be clear that consensus is more important in these societies than institutional integration and that this is partly responsible – especially in the least differentiated societies – for the prevalence of social order. Lastly, we do not mean to suggest that these societies are socially just in every respect. It is only in so far as they are reciprocative and open that they are more just than societies characterised by exploitation and centres closed to their peripheries. It is to a consideration of the latter type of society that we now turn.

111

7 Studies in Order, Reform and Revolution – II

In the present chapter we continue our studies in order, reform and revolution with an examination of societies characterised by inequality and exploitation. We deal first with those without an effective cultural system controlled by the dominant centres and then with societies with hegemonic centres.

Inequality and Exploitation

Inequality and exploitation are compatible with social order provided there is hegemonic control over the cultural system; in the absence of hegemony there will be a pattern of intermittent and more or less radical dissent that is derogated or proscribed by the centre. Just as in other types of society this situation is rarely realised in pure form. But this pattern is present in many more societies and it is inherent as an emergent pattern in all societies. The stability of societies in which this pattern is dominant is particularly dependent on the balance of power between the contending forces and we must therefore pay particular attention to the emergent contradictions within and among different forces and relations of production. To illustrate the dynamics of dissent in this type of society, therefore, we shall first examine the different historical bureaucratic empires.

The historic empires had attained a high level of structural differentiation relative to the societies – whether patrimonial, conquest or feudal – from which they had emerged and had also developed sufficient free-floating or generalised resources to support a centralised bureaucracy. The empires were characterised by political centralisation under a comparatively autonomous centre controlled by the emperor and the bureaucracy. Although they were based, like the African kingdoms considered above, on a traditional legitimation, they also frequently developed wider, potentially universal political and cultural orientations that transcended the particularisms of subordinate groups, classes or strata. There were clearly considerable variations in these systems in the

112

relative strength of different power centres and a correspondingly wide variation in the pattern of dissent and disorder. Their dynamics also depended on the precise character of the super-imposition or conjuncture of the different inherent and emergent contradictions and also on the impact of external powers and exogenous factors.[1] The vastly different histories of England, France, Russia, China, the Ottoman Empire, Spain and India are adequate testimony to the importance of such variations and it is clearly beyond the scope of this monograph to consider all these systems.

The contradictions of the African kingdoms are present in the empires in more acute and more advanced form and are com-bined with yet other contradictions. The two major foci of emergent contradictions were rooted in the needs of the political centre to overcome the inherent contradictions in its relations with other systems. The political centre had both to develop free-floating or generalised resources to implement its policies and also to subordinate all potentially autonomous groups or systems. Secondly, the political centre needed to undermine the power of the hereditary, traditional aristocracy and its localised bases of support and at the same time maintain its own traditional legiti-mation. The precise manner in which these contradictions were resolved had important implications for the development of the empires.

The limited technological development of these societies enforced a policy of encouraging different groups, classes and social strata to provide free-floating, non-embedded resources for political purposes. Failure to develop these resources or their exhaustion through wasteful or unsuccessful political policies meant an increasing dependence on conservative and traditional groups that controlled embedded resources and especially land and rural manpower. Conversely successful development of the groups, classes or strata able to provide more generalised resources typically led to their autonomy and potential opposition to the political centre in a system characterised by increasing power incongruencies. This opposition appears in the autonomous ten-dencies and the non-traditional and dissensual orientations of merchants, financiers, industrialists, religious and educational institutions, and even the bureaucracy itself. Similarly in the stratification system the political centre tried to limit the power of aristocratic and land-holding groups and to create new, dependent and loyal strata; but the latter usually became aristo-

113

cratised themselves owing to the centre's reliance on traditional values in the attribution of status (e.g. the *noblesse de robe*). Yet if the centre went beyond traditional criteria of legitimation and status attribution, it necessarily undermined its own legitimacy and prestige. The emphasis on traditional status had further contradictory implications – especially in the overvaluation of land relative to generalised capital and in the inability of the political centre to appeal to the periphery in non-traditional terms against either the aristocracy or emergent autonomous strata. There were further, although less fundamental, conflicts and contradictions in other policies and their impact on the power and exchange relations within these imperial systems. But their general nature should be clear from the preceding account and we now turn to a specific illustration.[2]

The Imperial Chinese system had a politico-cultural centre in which the bureaucracy and literati were more or less equal in power and were involved in complex interdependencies. At the local level the Chinese village was less self-regulating than the Indian village community and was subject to both gentry and bureaucratic control. The literati provided the main link between the gentry and the bureaucracy through the system of open and competitive examinations held by the government. Scholars who wished to enter the imperial service were supported by their extended family or clan groups and the successful candidate recouped the outlay and often expanded it through the legitimate and illegitimate returns of office. In the absence of successful scholarship the wealth of family or clan (which at least among the lower gentry was largely derived from rents) would soon be dissipated through the system of equal inheritance of land. Examination and office were thus significant bases of economic as well as social, political and cultural power.

The bulk of the imperial revenue even in the mid-nineteenth century and even more of the local and provincial revenues derived from the land-tax and the sanctions for its collection were military and bureaucratic in nature rather than religious, as in the Indian system. The imperial government was thus interested in maintaining control over the rural population as a means of extracting its share of the agricultural surplus; and the gentry had a similar interest in the continuing power of the government. The latter also ran the examination system. This served not only as a means of bureaucratic recruitment but also as a means of socialisation into the central value system and as a means of controlling status attribution. Indeed the importance of the examination system in imperial control can be seen in the reaction to government threats to suspend examinations in a recalcitrant district. However, this system was undermined by the government's resort to the sale of degrees in an attempt to raise revenue in the wake of the Taiping Rebellion and the system was eventually abolished in 1905. This in turn led to an increase in the prestige attached to Western education and thereby to a radicalisation of student and official strata.

These contradictions in the examination system were just one manifestation of the more general contradiction that emerged during the development of the Manchu dynasty in the later part of the nineteenth century. This more general contradiction took the form of a conflict between the need to increase revenues to suppress internal rebellion and face foreign enemies and the need to maintain the power of the gentry class with which the literati and bureaucracy were so closely connected. Foreign domination of commercial trade and the unequal treaties limited the scope for mobilising revenues from trade; but an increase in the government's share of the agricultural surplus would undermine the base of the scholar-gentry class. Moreover, the latter had previously controlled the emergent urban commercial class through heavy taxation and state monopolies (e.g. salt trade) and thus the indigenous bourgeoisie was weakened. The continuing prestige of the scholar-gentry strata also encouraged the emergent urban commercial classes to invest their capital in land, examinations or degrees. This further limited the government's opportunities for confronting the internal and external threats to its stability. Accordingly it relied increasingly on local gentry and military leaders to put down peasant rebellions and thus initiated a progressive decentralisation of political power that eventually led to the overthrow of the imperial dynasty in the Revolution of 1911.

The gentry were more oriented to the cultivation of literature than land and they were also more exploitative than landlords in England or Japan or Mogul India. This was particularly so in the nineteenth and twentieth centuries. The relations between gentry and peasantry were thus particularly prone to dissent and disorder and there was a celebrated tradition of peasant rebellion throughout China. The typical pattern of strains underlying these rebellions included a period of crop-failure and famine in combination with excessive oppression and extortion by local gentry and officials and with a general failure to provide protection from bandits and warlords. These rebellions were intermittent and most were limited in radicalism although they typically combined political with religious orientations. The additional aggravations imposed by population growth, imperial decline, foreign political and economic penetration, and increasing exploitation, contributed to an even more disorderly period of relations in the late nineteenth and early twentieth centuries. There was increasing pauperisation and an actual decline in the area under cultivation during this period. In the south landlords were taking up to seventy or eighty per cent of the crop by the 1930s; and in the wheat-growing north, where peasant proprietorship was more widespread, usurious interest rates were a major source of complaint. Conditions were thus highly conducive to peasant mobilisation and required only freedom from repression and the right strategy on the part of radical cadres to provide the base of a radical revolutionary movement.

The continuing decline of the empire was marked by the various unequal treaties imposed by the Western powers and by military defeat at the hands of the Japanese in 1895. The latter finally discredited the gentry and officials who had attempted to arrest the imperial decline through strengthening the gentry and introducing minor reforms. A modern nationalist movement developed and appealed particularly to students and intellectuals. The young emperor himself was converted to a programme of radical reform in 1898 but this was opposed successfully by the domineering Empress Dowager. When the Boxer Rebellion broke out in 1900 with an anti-dynastic and xenophobic ideology the Empress Dowager was able to deflect its violence against the foreigners and reformist officials who were under the influence of foreign ideas. However, the rebels were eventually defeated by foreign troops and further indemnities were imposed by the colonial powers. Following this defeat attempts at reform and constitutional government were made but these were ineffective and failed to stem the decline.

The Ch'ing dynasty established by the Manchu conquerors was overthrown by the Revolution of 1911. This was ostensibly effected by the liberal Sun Yat-sen's revolutionary movement of students, anti-Manchu secret societies, overseas Chinese, soldiers and officials. But the liberal movement lacked mass support and its success was due in large measure to the support of warlords and gentry who wished for the end of Manchu government. The leading warlord, Yuan Shih-k'ai, assumed the Presidency of the Republic and later attempted to establish a new dynasty. He was deposed in 1915 by other warlords because he failed to resist the Twenty-One Demands of the Japanese with sufficient vigour. His deposition initiated an eleven-year period of warlord rule throughout China in which coercion was the dominant base of power and in which the peasantry and urban periphery were subject to increasing exploitation. The warlords used their military power to exact revenues from the government and from each other, from the merchants and peasants, from officials and gentry alike. In the countryside warlords and gentry increased rents and interest rates, demanded taxes many years in advance, raised military corvées, and contributed to inflation through the issue of irredeemable paper money. At the same time peasant handicraft industries went into decline and dykes and irrigation channels were left to deteriorate. The government failed to stimulate economic growth and relied on foreign loans; most of its expenditure was in the military sphere. The warlord period was thus one of increasing and flagrant inequality and exploitation and saw a corresponding increase in dissent at both the periphery and the marginal centre.

The early stages of the warlord period none the less saw some rapid industrial development stimulated by the First World War and its concomitant fall in imports. The emergent urban bourgeoisie tended at first to ally with the gentry and invested much of its capital in land; later it allied in large part with the reformed Kuomintang (K.M.T.). The proletariat formed labour movements which initially were simply mutual-aid societies but which became more radical under deteriorating conditions and the leadership of intellectuals. The establishment of Japanese domination in Manchuria was consolidated after the First World War and provoked a sharp reaction against both Japan and her Chinese sympathisers. At the same time the Russian Revolution had a significant impact on radicals in China and led to the emergence of a reformed K.M.T. under Sun Yat-sen and the establishment of the independent Republican government at Canton (which was none the less dependent on warlord support for its stability). The Chinese Communist Party (C.C.P.) was formed in 1921 with Comintern assistance and it entered an alliance with the K.M.T. and itself began attempts to mobilise the new proletariat in northern China. However, the succession of Chiang K'ai-shek to the leadership of the Kuomintang following the death of Sun Yat-sen in 1925 led to preparations for a purge of the Communists. This purge came in 1927 and many Communists and workers were killed. From then on the K.M.T. was increasingly allied with imperialist, merchant and landlord interests.

Under Comintern influence the C.C.P. had maintained the alliance with the K.M.T. until the purge and had also concentrated its energies in the organisation of the urban proletariat rather than the peasantry. Between 1924 and 1927 they had considerable success in this respect owing to the impact of the world recession and the nationalist reaction sparked by foreign shootings of Chinese on 30 May 1925. The Communists were also influential in peasant unrest, starting with rebellions in East Kwangtung in the early 1920s. The Northern Expedition led by Chiang K'ai-shek in 1925 to expel the warlords to the north of Kwangtung also included many Communists and met with considerable success throughout central and eastern China. It was after this success that Chiang launched his purge of the first United Front, established a new Republic centred on Nanking, and entered alliances with the northern warlords. After the initial establishment of the new Nationalist Republic Chiang's main conflicts were with other warlords but he began to turn his attention once more to the Communists and mass movements in 1932.

Further Communist uprisings after the Nationalist purge were ineffective (e.g. Nanchang, Autumn Harvest) but Mao Tse-tung did establish a base area in the Hunan-Kiangsi-Fukien region. Communist success here was due largely to the beneficence of Soviet economic, political and social policies and to the effectiveness of the Red armies and propaganda. Soviets developed wherever Communist armies were able to keep out White armies through superior military force. The Red armies in turn received mass support from the peasants and recruited from the large pool of secret society members, enemy soldiers, bandits and similar *elements declasses* in the region. The Communists developed not only military power but also economic self-sufficiency.

But by 1934 not only had the C.C.P. been largely eradicated in the towns but the Nationalist armies had also destroyed or were encircling all the Communist rural Soviets. This situation led to the Long March from Kiangsi to the Shensi Soviet in the north. The C.C.P. failure to mobilise sufficient support to resist Nationalist attack led to a reorientation of policy and a call for

118

a second united front with the K.M.T. against the Japanese. The C.C.P. also made concessions to the middle-class and rich peasantry insisting only on rent reductions and not on the distribution of land other than that owned by large and middle landowners. The increasing hostility towards the Japanese following the attempt to establish an Autonomous North Chinese State forced Chiang K'ai-Shek to enter a second united front with the C.C.P. But there was a rapid deterioration of relations that resulted in a blockade of the Communist areas and to open military clashes.

Within the K.M.T.-controlled areas, however, there was a two-hundred-fold inflation during the course of the war and the burden of the war was inequitably distributed. The failure to protect the salaries of the middle class and intellectuals and the favour shown to landlords rather than middle and poor peasants deprived the Nationalists of much popular support. In contrast the beneficient policies and military protection provided by the C.C.P. encouraged such support for the Communists. Between 1937 and 1945 the Red Army increased from about 80,000 to more than half a million, the number of party members rose from about 100,000 to a million, and the areas under Communist power and influence grew from half of Shansi to most of northern and eastern China outside the major cities.

The war clearly played a crucial role in the mobilisation of Communist support but it is open to debate whether it was essential to the success of the Communist revolution. The Revolution of 1911 merely removed the imperial dynasty; it did nothing about the other structural conflicts and contradictions present in the imperial system. The period of warlordism following the liberal revolution was one of increasing inequality and exploitation and of increasing discontent. The success of the radical movements of this period (especially the Northern Expedition and the Soviets of 1928–1930) suggest that sooner or later a natural disaster would combine with falling rural standards to create the conditions for a successful guerrilla campaign against K.M.T. forces. The Sino-Japanese war was important because it provided an earlier opportunity for such a campaign and because it added urban, Nationalist support to that of rural discontent. The economic and social policies of the Communists and their nationalist sympathies were in any event sufficient to tip the military balance in favour of the revolutionary movement and against the Nationalist republican government.[3]

119

The Chinese empire illustrates the pattern of intermittent and more or less radical dissent characteristic of systems based on exploitation and inequality. It was eventually overthrown by a combination of forces when its emergent contradictions had already caused its virtual extinction. Thereafter the period of warlordism saw a continuation of exploitation and inequality in which Communist and Nationalist forces fought, sometimes in alliance and sometimes in opposition, for the control of the peasantry. The eventual success of the Red armies was due to the relative beneficence of Soviet rule in conjunction with the progressive deterioration of Nationalist power owing to its inherent and emergent contradictions. The Communists took advantage of the decline of the warlord system and the Japanese invasion to alter the balance of power through the establishment of indedent political, economic, social and cultural bases from which to launch a final assault on the Nationalist power systems. Thus the Communist revolution resolved one set of contradictions and substituted a different set whose consequences are still being worked out.

We now turn to a consideration of a case intermediate between the exploitative and inegalitarian system and the hegemonic and exploitative system. This case is that of the six counties of Ulster. An examination of its structure and the pattern of dissent will provide an answer to some of the questions posed in our first chapter and also provide a partial illustration of an hegemonic society.

Ulster is characterised by a strong politico-economic centre mediated by social and cultural power based on religious affiliations. The nature of the dominant centre derives from the historical context of Irish colonisation and the subsequent partition of Ireland into an independent Catholic south and a dependent Protestant north. We need to review this history in order to understand the present disorders.

At the start of the sixteenth century Ireland was a largely autonomous, decentralised, agricultural and pastoral Catholic society. But its opposition to English influence and its involvement in international power politics led thenceforth to the increasing settlement of English Protestant landlords and lowland Scots Presbyterian colonists. This plantation of Ireland was sponsored by the English state and, particularly in the later period of settlement, conducted by private speculators who 'undertook' to provide tenants for land confiscated from Irish and Anglo-Irish landowners. Such tenants were less easy to find than 'undertakers' and so the Irish were permitted to remain in large numbers as tenants. There was intermittent organised resistance to this settlement throughout the sixteenth and seventeenth centuries and this resistance was particularly strong in both Ulster and Wexford. All the rebellions were sooner or later suppressed and by the end of the seventeenth century almost all the land was owned by a new Protestant Ascendancy. Ulster was settled later than many other areas and it had not only a greater proportion of immigrant settlers but also a distinctive pattern of tenure that encouraged improvement and cash cropping. The new Protestant ruling class proceeded to consolidate its position through enactment of a penal code designed to prevent the Catholics obtaining property, influence, political or cultural power. There was also discrimination against dissenting denominations. Thus the religious conflicts of the sixteenth and seventeenth centuries were superimposed on, and articulated with, the political and economic conflicts created by the settlement of Ireland.

Increasing population in the eighteenth century led not only to pressure on land and higher rents but also to urban growth and industrial development. In rural areas this accentuated the tripartite division between Anglican landlords, Presbyterian tenants and Catholic tenants. Agrarian secret societies were formed to impose rent and tithe reductions and to intimidate economic rivals of opposed religions. These societies included the precursors of the Orange movement which was later to be employed by the ruling class to resist opposition and to divide the periphery along sectarian lines. There were similar conflicts between Catholic and Protestant workers in the towns. But there was also a conflict between the Presbyterian urban bourgeoisie and the Anglican landed gentry. This latter conflict resulted in the formation of United Irish movements of middle-class Catholic and radical dissent in opposition to gentry rule and in favour of liberal nationalism. The ineffective United Irish revolt in 1798 was repressed and precipitated the Act of Union and the abolition of the Irish parliament. The repression of this movement was greatly assisted by government encouragement of sectarianism.

During the nineteenth century both sectarian conflicts and co-operation across religious groups continued. A middle-class Catholic emancipation movement in the early part of the century

121

mobilised both peripheral Catholic and middle-class Presbyterian support. Later in the century there developed non-sectarian economic movements to protect and improve tenants' rights and urban workers' conditions and wages. There were also non-sectarian nationalist and cultural movements. Agitation for land reform was often combined with, and later contained within, the agitation for Irish home rule. The more radical manifestations of economic, political, social and cultural deprivation were derogated or proscribed by the Catholic hierarchy and the Protestant establishment alike. But the demand for home rule received support from both the Catholic bishops (hence the fear of 'Rome rule') and the Liberal administrations of the late nineteenth century. Opposition to the Home Rule movement came from the landed gentry primarily but they were able to mobilise sectarian resistance from the Protestant periphery. This resistance was naturally strongest in Ulster (although even here the nine counties were evenly divided between Unionists and Nationalists) and it was the Ulster issue that dominated the conflict.

The various delays in granting home rule encouraged the development of movements which sought independence through violent or non-violent resistance rather than legislative means (e.g. Sinn Fein and the Irish Republican Brotherhood) and simultaneously provided the opportunity to organise resistance to home rule in Ulster. The First World War caused a further delay and precipitated a civil war in which the vast majority of the Catholic population came to support the Sinn Fein and its guerrilla movement. The solution finally adopted was an unworkable compromise that pleased few interests and involved the partition not only of Ireland as a whole but also of Ulster itself. Three largely Catholic counties were incorporated into the Irish Free State and the remaining six counties – not all with Protestant majorities – were included within Northern Ireland. In both the Free State and Northern Ireland civil wars continued and in both the balance of power favoured the more conversative governments rather than the republican movement.

In the six counties of contemporary Northern Ireland there is a major conflict between the Unionist and the Catholic blocs. The Unionist bloc includes the landowners, the industrial bourgeoisie, the Protestant urban petit-bourgeoisie, the Protestant working and peasant classes. It has been led historically by the landowning class, united by its commitment to Protestantism and integrated by the Orange institutions. The political and

122

economic centre is able to dominate this alliance through its control over both policy benefits and economic rewards and through its social and cultural power which elicits deference and continued commitments. Its control over the government as well as the Apprentice Boys of Derry, the Royal Black Preceptory, and similar organisations, facilitates the exchange of housing, employment, educational opportunities, upward social mobility, etc., for political support and influence. There are none the less important and increasing conflicts within the Unionist bloc: between landed and industrial interests, Church of Ireland and Presbyterian interests, and between centre and periphery. These conflicts are associated with the emergent contradictions in the power structure and will be discussed below. Opposed to the Unionist bloc is a Catholic bloc which is less organised and largely disfranchised (either directly or through gerrymandering). Within the Catholic bloc we find the Nationalist Party with its politics of clerical conservatism and based on Catholic tenant farmers, landowners and agricultural labour; the Northern Ireland Labour Party and the Republican Labour Party based largely on the urban working class; and the Irish Republican Army, now split into a Provisional Council (of traditional 'green' republicans) and an I.R.A. rump of socialist revolutionaries. The Catholic hierarchy is still influential over the Catholic bloc and counsels moderation and accommodation; while the Ancient Order of Hibernians performs for Catholics services similar to those performed by Orange institutions for Unionists. Both Catholic and Unionist leaders have employed sectarian commitments to disrupt economic and political movements that mobilised working class or peasantry along non-sectarian class lines (e.g. in the late nineteenth century, in the industrial movements of 1906 and the 1930s).

The extent of discrimination against Catholics is a subject of much debate but its existence has been recognised by various official bodies as well as other observers. Evidence as to discrimination can be found in the allocation of council housing, in central and local government employment, in the incidence of unemployment and income distribution figures, in economic development policies (rationalisation and investment favouring counties east of the River Bann and hence largely Protestant counties); in the drawing of electoral boundaries, in educational policy (ranging from state support of primary schools to the location of the new University of Ulster), in police enrolment and

123

the administration of justice, in other political policy benefits; in the attribution of status and deference; and in the central value system. In their turn the Catholic community practise various forms of religious exclusiveness – educational, marital, commercial, political, housing, social, and so forth. The pattern of discrimination is qualified in one respect through the implementation of welfare-state policies by the Stormont government and the concomitant subsidies from the Westminster government. This alleviates somewhat the economic and social discrimination against Catholics and has also reduced the pressure towards emigration.

The dominant centre in Northern Ireland is a political and economic centre in which political power is essential to the continuance of economic exploitation at current levels but not necessarily to the maintenance of economic power *per se*. The maintenance of power is complicated by the economic, political, social and cultural interrelations with the centres and periphery of the rest of the United Kingdom and by the increasing importance of foreign investment. The religious organisations are also important, if weaker, central powers and the Catholic hierarchy is particularly important in this respect for its control over the Catholic periphery. Within the periphery there are significant economic, political, social and cultural conflicts and religious affiliation tends to coincide with these conflicts (e.g. skill levels, policy benefits, status, educational opportunities). The inherent tendencies towards religious conflict in this situation are encouraged (albeit for different reasons) by both Unionist and Catholic hierarchies. Religious conflict is thus inevitable within the present power structure and pattern of exploitation and not all its manifestations receive central approbation.

The inherent contradictions and conflicts of interest in the distribution of power and pattern of exchange relations are thus associated with diverse dissensual movements. But these will not themselves cause a radical change in the pattern of domination unless there is a drastic shift in the balance of power between the contending forces. There are indeed several dynamic forces operating to produce such a shift, ranging from differential population growth to the intervention of the Westminster government. But the most significant of such forces are the emergent contradictions in the structure of economic and political power within the six counties themselves. There is an increasingly acute contradiction within the economic and political systems between the need to attract industrial investment and long-term orders and the need to maintain a system of power and exploitation that precipitates conflict and thereby discourages investment. This contradiction is aggravated by the inherent contradictions within the Unionist bloc between the landowners and the industrial bourgeoisie and also between the Church of Ireland and the Presbyterian faithful. For industrial development threatens the interests of the landed gentry in so far as the latter is not linked to the bourgeoisie; and concessions to the Catholic community and the more general extension of civil rights create a backlash from the Presbyterian periphery in defence of its interests in the *status quo*. Such concessions and the economic improvement will further discourage Catholic emigration and so accelerate the changing population balance that also threatens the maintenance of the present power system. The economic and political policies of the Stormont government thus contradict the maintenance of its power and also create disorder unfavourable to the continuance of its economic policies. At the same time there has developed a civil rights movement based on an alliance of Catholic professional and bourgeois classes oriented to upward economic, political and social mobility, of radical non-sectarian students from Queen's University and other educational institutons, and thirdly of more peripheral Catholics oriented to employment and housing opportunities. This movement also has support from Protestant middle-class individuals and from British politicians. It has been treated as a sectarian movement and has evoked a violent response from both the police and the Protestant periphery. The future stability of Northern Ireland is dependent on the extent to which the industrial bourgeoisie are able to isolate, either simultaneously or consecutively, the radical elements in the civil rights movement and the radical Protestant backlash and thus to preserve both the economic policies and the image of order and progress essential to the maintenance of its power. This in turn depends on the validity of the recent concessions of electoral reform, police reorganisation and disarmament, local government reform based on fewer councils and more limited powers, the Commissioner for Complaints, the Prevention of Incitement to Hatred Act, the regional housing commission, and so forth; and on the ability to contain both the radical Protestant and the radical non-sectarian movements and so ensure at least a pragmatic acquiescence in the structure of power while these reforms are carried out. The prospects for an end to social

125

and political disorder and even more the prospects for social justice are obviously dependent on more radical changes in the distribution of power and the pattern of exchange.[4]

Northern Ireland provides an illustration of the disorder generated in an inegalitarian and exploitative system in which the cultural power of the centre is only partially effective. Dissent is inevitable in such a society and its form corresponds well with the general model outlined above. The extensive power congruency has prevented successful 'strike' action against the economic and political centre and thereby the creation of a less exploitative system. In this respect the cultural division between Catholics and Protestants within the periphery has helped to ensure an alternative supply of contributions to the two major power systems. This division has also enabled the centre to divert dissent towards peripheral scapegoats and towards the comparatively weak Catholic hierarchy; and to repress the Catholic periphery through the 'misguided' loyalties of the regular police and special constabulary. On the other hand the cultural division within the society has strengthened the power of the Catholic hierarchy and also provided a permanent source of dissent against the structure of power in Northern Ireland. It is thus impossible to avoid dissent and disorder against the dominant political and economic centre even if scapegoating and repression have enabled the system to survive more or less intact since 1922.

But the recent emergence of contradictions within and between the dominant power systems has meant an increasing amount of dissent and disorder. The emergent contradiction between the political and economic centres is rooted in the conflicting needs to attract outside investment and to maintain a structure of power that generates disorder. This contradiction is reflected within the political centre in the conflicts between landed and industrial interests (e.g. O'Neill versus Faulkner) and in the conflicts between the reformist and the more traditionalist interests. The reforms introduced by the centre in response to the demands of political movements and of economic growth have been interpreted as betrayals of the values previously espoused and this has generated a backlash against both the reformers and the 'revolutionary' movement responsible. The concessions have thus involved a weakening of the Unionist hegemony and revealed an inflexibility in its cultural system. These have been exploited by Paisley and others who claim greater integrity in their commitment to the dominant values of Protestant Unionism. Thus the

126

economic policies of O'Neill and his successors, Chichester-Clark and Faulkner, have created a vicious circle of disorder in which both concession and the refusal of concession generate further disorder. The standpoints of the reformer, the reactionary and the revolutionary in such a situation are thus equally imposed by the dynamics of the dominant power systems and their emergent contradictions. The outcome will depend on the decisions made by these three elements and their relevance to the continuing economic, political, social and cultural changes.

Exploitation and Hegemony

We now turn to our third type of society characterised by an extensive social order. This is one in which exploitation is important but where there is a sufficiently strong and effective cultural power system that ensures acquiescence in the continuing operation of dominant institutions. The stability of social order in such societies depends on the flexibility and effectiveness of the cultural system and on the degree of control over alternative bases of cultural power. Where the cultural system is inflexible then change must be rigorously controlled to coincide with institutionalised expectations and commitments. If deprivation is still experienced, it must be channelled away from the centre itself and towards the periphery or other scapegoats. Such a society becomes unstable when the cultural system is ineffective and the dominant centres are subject to emergent contradictions that prevent the maintenance of control through the use of more concrete situational sanctions. It is thus necessary to examine not only the legitimation processes but also the structural dynamics of such societies in order to understand their relative stability and orderliness.

Hegemony can truly be said to exist only where there is an inegalitarian and exploitative system in which the periphery as well as the centre is committed to the central value system. We can therefore identify hegemony where the existence of exploitation is either denied by the periphery and/or accepted as inevitable or legitimate so that radical dissent is either not articulated or its repression is also accepted as legitimate. There are clearly many societies in which such hegemony is at least partly realised, and especially in its pragmatic acquiescence form of inevitability. But there is considerable evidence that this is the situation on a more widespread basis in many contemporary

127

Western societies where significant participation in the exercise of power is possible only at the cost of socialisation into the central value system.[5]

Contemporary Western societies vary somewhat in the relative autonomy and importance of different systems and in the goals and orientations of different centres. But they are all characterised by predominantly capitalist economies and in most cases by liberal democratic political systems and secularised central values. They also have highly advanced technologies for the creation, interpretation and specification of the dominant values. Hegemony is created and maintained, not through the operation of cultural institutions such as the family system, universal primary education, the churches and mass media, alone; but through the operation of all dominant institutions whether they have cultural primacy or not. The conscious co-ordination of these various agencies in the maintenance of hegemony is unnecessary provided there is a moderately high level of institutional integration and the different power systems are producing 'expected' levels of output. For in such circumstances the sheer weight of institutional inertia and the realisation of the participants' 'legitimate' expectations ensure that the dominant institutions and patterns of exchange are not only accepted as given or inevitable but are also accepted as proper and legitimate.[6] It is for this reason that emergent contradictions within and between the different power systems are so important in the generation of radical dissent – for they affect both the flow of rewards to the periphery and the degree of institutional integration between centres.

Thus the stability of such societies depends on the level of institutional integration and cultural-system effectiveness and on the ability of the different power systems to 'deliver the goods' expected by their participants. In a stable system these factors combine to produce peripheral acquiescence in the general structure of power and exchange relations and to ensure the continuation of 'realistic' expectations and 'negotiable' demands on the part of the periphery. Peripheral dissent in such a system thus typically involves a re-specification of dominant values and is limited to 'trade-union'-conscious demands for marginal redistributions of rewards and/or minor changes in the pattern of power and exchange relations. Provided the centres concede such demands or are able to justify their refusal then their hegemony and the relative passivity of the periphery will both be reinforced. Failure to concede such demands and to justify their refusal,

128

particularly when they are couched in terms of dominant values, often leads to the escalation of dissent and the combination of previously fragmented interests into more radical movements that question the legitimacy of the dominant institutions and exchange relations. As long as these more radical movements confine themselves to institutionalised modes of dissent they can be tolerated, since success is dependent on central approbation and the constraints of institutional inertia will ensure the continuing operation of the basic structures of power and exchange. It is where radical movements adopt uninstitutionalised methods (typically those that undermine or disrupt these basic structures) that they will be derogated or proscribed. It is precisely because radical but institutionalised dissent is compatible with the continuing operation of the basic structures of power and exploitation that it can be tolerated in such societies. In turn the very toleration of such movements and the institutional constraints operate to emasculate radicalism and to initiate a cycle of goal displacement.

Thus the extensive structural differentiation, the productivity of the differentiated systems and the secular culture of such societies are all particularly favourable to the maintenance of hegemony and the toleration of dissent. The extensive structural differentiation fragments interests and the secular culture permits these fragmented interests to find expression in reform movements oriented to a re-specification of dominant values and institutions. The fragmentation of interests combines with the unequal distribution of resources and the 'logic of collective action' to produce a system of imperfect competition in which there are many countervailing interests at intermediate levels of power and many checks against radical reforms from more powerful interests.[7] At the same time the expression of dissent in terms of dominant values reinforces the legitimacy of the total system even if it also means moderate reforms in particular structures of power and exchange. In their turn the stability and legitimacy thus maintained enable the continuing expansion of production in the different power systems and a continuing increase in the absolute levels of reward going to the periphery. Thus there is a virtuous circle of power and exchange processes that maintains the legitimacy, effectiveness and stability of these Western capitalist systems.

Yet the presence of significant marginal centres and of various groups outside the hegemonic consensus (e.g. ethnic minorities, pariah classes, immigrant groups) implies the omnipresence of more

129

or less radical dissent even in the absence of institutional mal-integration and emergent contradictions. This will be tolerated as long as it is expressed in terms of dominant values and/or confined to institutionalised channels of dissent. Indeed it may also be successful if it gains support from those with access to strategic resources or is associated with the opportunity for effective and legitimate strike action. These points are illustrated in Negro movements such as the National Association for the Advancement of Coloured Peoples with its legislative and judicial programme and the more accommodative Tuskegee movement led by Booker T. Washington. Even movements that adopt less approved methods but are committed to the dominant institutions and values may be tolerated provided that their targets are peripheral scapegoats. Movements with significant marginal centre support such as McCarthyism and John Birchism provide good examples of these 'reform' movements. But if such dissent takes uninstitutionalised form (e.g. non-violent civil disobedience or armed insurrection) and expresses hostility to dominant values then it will be repressed and its repression accepted as legitimate by other members of society. The Black Power movements in the U.S.A. and violent student movements in all Western societies illustrate such a reaction on the part of both centre and periphery. When such an escalation of dissent and adoption of illegitimate methods coincide with the development of emergent contradictions then there is increasing disorder and instability. But the balance of power is generally more than adequate to maintain stability despite increasing disorder and the pressures of institutional inertia and hegemony typically constrain a return to normalcy and order. The importance of these factors in the maintenance of stability is illustrated in the collapse of the British General Strike in 1926, the peripheral response to the economic depression of the 'thirties, and the Gaullist electoral victory following the collapse of the so-called French Revolution of 1968. Such moments are more significant indicators of the strength of hegemony than the more frequently cited examples of 'trade-union' consciousness or economism and the considerable working-class vote for conservative and clerical parties.[8]

The very fact that the General Strike and the May Events took place do none the less suggest that hegemony is never completely institutionalised in Western capitalist society. In addition to the various marginal centres and the groups outside the hegemonic consensus we find pockets of radical dissent within the periphery itself. Thus the periphery is not only committed to the dominant institutions but also affirms populist assumptions about the legitimate distribution of power. Likewise the periphery accepts the general legitimacy of the total economic, political and stratification systems but also rejects them in more specific, immediate contexts. These inconsistencies are typical of peripheries in hegemonic systems. Their experience of inequality and exploitation in everyday life contradicts the assumptions and assertions of the dominant value systems but their acceptance of these assumptions and assertions is none the less conditioned by manifold social relations, institutional constraints and cultural pressures.[9] This conflict is normally manifested in trade-union-conscious dissent but it may also develop into more radical protest when combined with institutional malintegration and emergent contradictions or when articulated by marginal centre groups. These processes are illustrated in the civil rights movement and the Protestant backlash in Northern Ireland and in the student-worker movement that developed in France in 1968. A further illustration is found in the dynamics of dissent in Weimar Germany and the subsequent accession to power of the Nazi Party.

Weimar Germany is clearly an imperfect example of hegemonic order and it is precisely because this is so that we can examine in its history the impact of breakdowns in hegemony in a pluralistic society subject to multiple emergent contradictions and institutional malintegration as well as more general dissensus.

Imperial Germany was dominated by a strong socio-political centre that encouraged and controlled her late, fast and thorough industrialisation for political ends. The dominance of the Prussian aristocracy and bureaucracy can be seen in the concern with national strength and unity rather than private profit in economic planning, in the development of state socialism and welfare policies, and in the 'nobilitation' of the emergent industrial and financial bourgeoisie. The periphery was excluded from substantial political power by the restricted franchise and dominant bureaucracy but it was none the less granted significant political and economic policy benefits and adopted a 'trade-union'-conscious ideology (especially in the Catholic and less inegalitarian south). The different power systems were thus well integrated and their hegemony survived despite economic and political vicissitudes until the German defeat in the First World War.

This defeat caused the destruction of the monolithic centre and the emergence of a pluralistic but malintegrated power structure. Thus the Weimar Constitution established a liberal democratic republic based on a universal franchise and proportional representation and thereby permitted the electoral success of left-wing and centrist coalition governments; while, at the same time, the bureaucracy and the numerically much reduced armed forces remained under the control of more aristocratic and conservative interests. The economy was likewise still dominated by the small interlocking industrial-financial cartels and monopolies and it still contained a significant labour-intensive, low-wage commercial and agricultural sector alongside the increasingly dominant capital-intensive, high-wage industrial sector. The stratification system was more pluralistic but rural *Junker* and military-bureaucratic status criteria remained important. In this way military defeat created not only institutional malintegration but also a structure of considerable power in congruencies between the polity and other power systems. These incongruencies were indeed initially associated with attempts to create the conditions for renewed social order – witness the *Arbeitsgemeinschaft* agreement reached between the employers and trade unions and also the *entente* between the military and the coalition government to circumvent and repress the revolutionary socialist movement. But such attempts were unsuccessful in the face of the general malintegration between the centres and the more immediate effects of the defeat.

Yet it is within this broad structural context that the more immediate effects of defeat and the later impact of hyperinflation and world-wide economic depression must be examined in order to understand the eventual success of the National Socialist movement. The Versailles Treaty imposed costly territorial, economic, military and social ('war-guilt') reparations on Germany and also reduced the size and power of the Armed Forces. It thus deprived Germany of heavy industrial areas and export markets, generated an influx of refugees from the ceded eastern territories, created a large force of demobilised and unskilled soldiers, weakened the monetary system and affronted the honour of the German nation in the eyes of its inhabitants. At the same time defeat liquidated millions of war loans floated by middle-class savings and precipitated revolutionary socialist and communist uprisings in Berlin, Munich and elsewhere. These deprivations and strains were worsened by international attempts to implement the

132

Versailles reparations and especially by the bilateral French and Belgian occupation of the Ruhr in 1923. It was the latter event that finally precipitated the notorious hyperinflation and concomitant economic collapse. It is hardly surprising to find these multiple contradictions and acute deprivations associated with the politicisation of interest articulation and the militarisation of political action as antagonistic classes, movements and strata attempted to maintain or seize power and/or to improve rewards or minimise losses. The most spectacular radical movements are found in the communist uprisings in Saxony and Thuringia and in the separatist and *volkisch* uprisings (including Hitler's beer-hall *putsch*) in Bavaria. But there were many other more or less radical, more or less violent, movements. Indeed the fragmentation of dissent was as important a factor in the maintenance of stability as the continuing balance of force in favour of the coalition government. There was a gradual return to social order following the stabilisation of the currency with the introduction of the *Rentenmark* and following the economic expansion generated by foreign loans and by the French evacuation of the Ruhr. But the bipolarisation of political support (witness the two 1924 elections) and the deprivations of these first five post-war years had a continuing and eventually disastrous impact.

The next six years were years of comparative economic prosperity during which economic development none the less served also to intensify the inherent and emergent contradictions within and between the social, political and economic systems. Economic expansion depended mainly on short-term international loans and was therefore vulnerable to all fluctuations in world trade and especially to the world-wide depression after 1929. Expansion also depended on industrial and commercial rationalisation and cartelisation and these processes adversely affected the significant *mittelstand* of retail traders, small businessmen and skilled craftsmen. Many of the middle class were living on proletarian incomes throughout this period and the 1929 depression subjected them to further acute economic and social deprivation. Educational expansion also generated deprivation for the middle classes since technical and university growth outpaced economic and political opportunities. The government continued to play an important role in economic development with its state sponsorship of rationalisation and cartelisation and with its encouragement of investment and the unions. But these policies antagonised the *petit bourgeoisie* and the government's deflationary policies

133

brought blame for low wages from the unions and for low prices from industry. Agriculture was afflicted by rural overpopulation, fluctuating markets and overproduction; the results were falling living standards, rural indebtedness (liquidated by hyperinflation but recreated by economic expansion) and falling prices. Moreover, these contradictions were exacerbated by the governmental policies of land settlement and discouragement of rural emigration. Thus there were important conflicts and contradictions in all sectors of the economy and these were compounded with similar strains in the political and the stratification systems.

The world depression that began in 1929 intensified these conflicts and contradictions and imposed acute deprivation on all classes and strata. Between the onset of depression and the end of 1932 unemployment rose from two million to six million, affecting proletariat and *mittelstand* alike; wages fell by a third while taxes rose *pari passu* to maintain the government's revenues; interest rates also rose to more than ten per cent; and agricultural prices fell further despite government aid. The political result was a renewed polarisation of party support and the rise on the right of the National Socialist Party. In the Reichstag the centre coalition governments were confronted by an obstructionist and intransigent bilateral opposition and normal legislation became so difficult that there was an increasing resort to government by decree. Moreover, these parliamentary conflicts were a pale reflection of the extra-parliamentary conflicts which were characterised by increasingly violent confrontations between radical right-wing paramilitary forces and radical working-class forces. The Nazi Party received financial support from the industrial cartels and military support from the Armed Forces – both of which were hostile to the government and fearful of a Bolshevik revolution. Its electoral strength derived primarily from the small-town and rural Protestant middle classes and particularly those who had previously voted for a centrist or regional party strongly opposed to big business and trade unions. Later it also gathered considerable support from new voters and previous non-voters, particularly women, as well as less extensive transfers from other parties. The Nazi Party organised skilful subcampaigns aimed at specific interests – fixed prices for farmers, jobs for the unemployed, liberation from competition for small businessmen, regeneration for the nationalists, careers for the young, and so forth – and did nothing that might antagonise financial or electoral support (until the 1932 elections when Hitler sacrificed financial support for electoral strength). Even so the Social Democrats retained most of its support and much of the transfer went to the communists; and the Centre Party also retained most of its heterogeneous support based on and mediated by religious commitment. The working class comprised half the population in 1933 and was too strong electorally to permit a majority vote for the Nazi Party and too weak to ensure a significant electoral defeat: and indeed the eventual Nazi success was due as much to intrigue about the President and to support from the economically and militarily powerful as to the electoral success among the periphery. Thus the post-war institutional malintegration was as necessary a factor in the apotheosis of Hitler as the economic, social and political conflicts that were the more immediate causes of his popular support. In contrast Britain's centre, for example, remained integrated and was able to maintain its hegemonic control throughout the (admittedly less severe) depression.

The National Socialists came to power constitutionally even if they had also engaged in much violent and derogated action before their accession to power. Moreover, it was through constitutional means that they proceeded to restructure the dominant patterns of power and exchange. These radical reforms (the so-called 'revolution from above') effected a reintegration of the different centres through the *Gleichschaltung* programme as well as the pacification of the periphery through the provision of material and symbolic rewards. The 'co-ordination' programme and the increasing effectiveness of the different power systems thus provided the conditions for the re-emergence of social order in an inegalitarian, exploitative and partially hegemonic system. While opposition was certainly repressed and 'subhuman' scapegoats were indubitably liquidated the overall result was social order on a wider scale than had been achieved except intermittently under the Weimar Constitution. The justice of such an order is an entirely different matter.[10]

The Nazi accession to power illustrates many of the tendencies characteristic of a pluralistic society subject to deflation in one or more power systems. These tendencies were intensified by the prior existence of extensive institutional malintegration between and within the different power systems. Events such as the hyper-inflation (which resulted in economic dislocation) and later the world depression led to intense conflict between central, marginal and peripheral interests as each tried to increase or maintain its share of power and rewards. Marginal groups and individuals developed radical solutions to these problems and sought more or less successfully to mobilise central and/or peripheral support behind these solutions.[11] The National Socialists were able to gather in this way the active or passive support of the economic, military and social centres; after the accession to power they also received support from the Catholic Centre Party by virtue of a concordat with the Vatican (cf. the similar arrangement agreed by Mussolini to facilitate the fascist rise to power). The political system was itself subject to internal malintegration – especially between the military and the executive, the federal and regional governments, and between the parties within the legislature – and during the depression each faction attempted to increase or maintain its power. There was an increasing resort to ultimate sanctions in all the systems and especially to the use of coercion in the political system. The balance of power and especially the balance of influence at the centre favoured the Nazi Party above other groups and thus led to the emergence of a new, strong political centre which proceeded to subordinate more or less successfully all other centres as well as the periphery.

In this section we have considered the nature of social order and disorder in societies characterised by inequality, exploitation and hegemony. We have pointed to the importance of structural differentiation, effective system performance and secularised culture in the maintenance of hegemony in Western capitalist societies; and also to the major sources of radical uninstitutionalised dissent. Lastly, we briefly described the rise of National Socialism in Germany to illustrate the dynamics of dissent in less integrated capitalist societies. It should be noted that even in Germany hegemony was a significant contributory factor in the rise of the Nazi movement – although the imperial political system was largely destroyed after the First World War, its hegemonic traditions survived both to increase the appeal of a radical movement that affirmed its commitment to traditional social and political values and also to weaken the opposition to Nazism from centrist and 'trade-union'-conscious parties. None the less the hegemonic appeal would have been insufficient in isolation to guarantee success: this required the depression and all those other conditions outlined above.

Further Reflections on Order and Stability

We turn finally to look at the conditions of order and stability in societies with differentiated and differentially strong centres. Even where there is differentiation in the strength of the economic, political, social and cultural centres, it is none the less rare to find that just one type of centre is dominant. It is more common to find two different but interdependent centres in a position of strength: neither capable of establishing and maintaining domination in isolation but together able to control the remaining centres and the periphery. Thus in nineteenth-century Britain it was a socio-economic centre that was dominant and in nineteenth-century Prussia it was a socio-political centre. In Northern Ireland we found a strong politico-economic centre and in Imperial China a strong politico-cultural centre. The Indian village community tended to be characterised by a dominant social and cultural centre. In contrast we find a comparatively strong political centre in the Third Reich and the Soviet Union; while there is a comparatively strong economic centre in the United States of America. In the following brief analysis we outline the general conditions of order and stability in societies with different dominant centres.

In a society with a *strong economic centre* economically powerful individuals and organisations are able to dominate other power systems either directly through an overlap of personnel or functions and/or indirectly through the market or through hegemonic commitments. Thus policy benefits will be disproportionately allocated in terms of economic criteria and access to prestigious roles or life-styles will depend on prior access to economic power and rewards. The cultural system will maintain long-term and inelastic commitments to continuing productivity and will legitimate the activities of the economic centre. There is an emphasis on market rationality in the distribution of system outputs rather than on substantive rules, irrespective of the costs and benefits involved. Money will be correspondingly important as a medium of exchange and the economic centre will attempt to extend its importance in the operation of other power systems. The continued strength of such a centre is thus critically dependent on the ability to control not only the economy but also the interrelations between different power systems (especially where these exchanges are mediated by money). Indeed the combination of sophisticated economic planning and the flexibility of money as a generalised medium in a world economy is an important source of economic dominance and facilitates the transcendence of emergent contradictions without fundamental change in the distribution of power between centre and periphery. A strong

137

economic centre is none the less vulnerable to contingencies that increase the importance of other sanctions and systems and also to emergent contradictions within the economy itself. Thus the outbreak of war tends to increase the autonomy of the military and political system and to extend the use of coercive sanctions in conflict with market rationality;[12] it may also extend the military participation ratio and impose new types of deprivation with consequences that are incompatible with the continuing strength of the economic centre. Likewise emergent contradictions within the economy (e.g. between increasing socialisation of the means of production and continuing private ownership of the means of production) and less fundamental processes such as deflation or inflation may also precipitate dissent and institutional malintegration. Provided this dissent can be diverted away from the economic centre to the periphery (e.g. trade-union aggressiveness) or to another centre (e.g. government taxation) then economic order can be maintained. Even economic disorder is compatible with continuing economic dominance, however, provided the other centres remain committed to the dominant centre and invoke their sanctions in its support. Since this is typically the case, the strong economic centre usually retains its flexibility and its dominance.

A society with a *strong political centre* is faced with somewhat different exigencies from those confronting the economically dominant centre. The political centre is based ultimately on control over negative sanctions and is thus critically dependent on the smooth functioning of those systems that produce positive sanctions and resources which can then be translated into policy benefits. But if this smooth functioning is to be compatible with continuing political domination then the operation of these other power systems must be mediated by authoritative sanctions and subject to extensive planning. Resources and rewards must be allocated according to politically rational criteria and not according to the ability to pay ('utility') or socially ascribed criteria.[13] In particular this means that a dominant political centre must also control the economic system and ensure the continuing supply of resources for the operation of the political system: in contrast, an economically dominant centre can operate under certain historical and structural conditions with only limited, *laissez-faire* government. The historical bureaucratic empires typically disintegrated or declined, for example, because they were either too repressive of economically active classes or allowed

138

them so many autonomy that these classes became increasingly dominant as well. The political system must also control the operations and resources of the other two power systems to ensure its legitimation and the integration of status and commitments with political power. Thus the persistence of traditional values and autonomous hereditary strata in the bureaucratic empires was a major restriction on the power of the emperors to control the attribution of status and to legitimate new institutions and policies. The Soviet and National Socialist political systems have been much more successful in this respect – the party controlling both status attribution (e.g. through the communist *nomenklatura* system[14]) and the cultural system with considerable effect. A final problem of particular importance in politically dominated societies is found in the relationship between military and civilian organisations, interests and values. Thus a strong military centre must subordinate the civilian bureaucracy or find its authority subverted and a strong civilian political centre must control not only the bureaucracy but also the military. Moreover, while the military can employ coercive sanctions against the bureaucracy, a civilian centre cannot employ these sanctions against the military as a whole and must therefore constrain obedience over at least a fraction of the military through other means (typically hegemonic commitments and economic inducements). Failure to maintain the loyalty of the military will necessarily expose civilian governments to *coups d'état* or to more radical revolutionary movements.

Thus it should be clear that the politically dominant centre is particularly vulnerable both to emergent contradictions between the political system and subordinate systems and also to internal contradictions and malintegration. Intersystemic contradictions can develop from emergent contradictions within these subordinate systems themselves and/or from inflationary and deflationary pressures originating in the political system. Thus an overextension of political goals relative to the capacities of other systems to provide the necessary inputs for goal attainment could precipitate dissent and political instability: military defeat and economic collapse are both important precursors of revolutionary movements. Conversely, an inadequate level of demand for the outputs of subordinate systems could lead to the investment of these outputs in increasing the power of such systems relative to the dominant political systems; the bureaucratic empires provide many illustrations of such emergent contradictions. It is for these reasons that efficient and flexible planning is so important to the continued strength of a politically dominant centre. Only when the operations and resources of other systems are regulated to meet the requirements of the political system can such domination be guaranteed. In this respect inefficient planning that precipitates not only political dissent but also undermines the efficacy and/or loyalties of the military is particularly maladroit since the power of the political centre depends in the last resort on a favourable balance of coercive power. Moreover, the victims of coercion cannot be indispensable to the smooth operation of the political system since coercion would otherwise be counterproductive. Thus, in so far as political planning is beset by uncertainties and inflexibilities, the political centre must be potentially less stable than economic centres with flexible market mechanisms and highly generalised media of exchange and co-ordination.

A society with a *strong social centre* is unlikely to exist in pure form but such a centre is often found in combination with a strong economic, political or cultural centre. It is unlikely because status depends on the predefinition of valued collectivities, roles and life-styles; and their value depends in turn on the relative dominance of other systems or on the ability of an independent social élite to control the cultural definitions of prestige. It is therefore most usual to find that social status is an important independent base for gaining access to other centres of power and for acquiring resources on favourable terms; in turn those with considerable power in other systems will attempt to translate their power and resources into social status through intermarriage or the acquisition of the prestigious life-style defined by the social élite. In a society with a truly strong social centre, however, the distribution of power and rewards would be totally determined by the social élite and not by a combination of social and non-social criteria. Each stratum would have prescribed rights and duties in each power system and there would be a high correlation between status and resources and rewards. The cultural system must be controlled by the socially prestigious so that an independent cultural centre cannot redefine the prestige hierarchy in its own favour; and the political system must be similarly controlled to ensure the implementation of the rights and duties attached to each stratum. Since the criterion for power and resource allocation is status, the centre must also eliminate or control the operation of economic markets and monetary systems so that an independent economic class of traders or entrepreneurs cannot emerge. Indeed the social centre would have to eliminate or incorporate all emergent bases of power outside the established structure or else face the possibility of revolutionary displacement. The need to incorporate emergent powerful interests implies the need for at least some social mobility and this too must be controlled by the social centre either directly through a sponsorship system or indirectly through the regulation of contest mobility. In this context it is advisable to have a multiplicity of strata so that the upward mobility of a successful stratum does not impose severe deprivation on a single displaced stratum but involves minor deprivations on many strata. Such a plurality of strata will also serve to fragment the interests of those intermediate in status between centre and extreme periphery and thus prevent a concerted opposition to the social centre. If the dominant centre is able to maintain its ideological hegemony and is sufficiently flexible to incorporate powerful emergent interests and to alter the stratification system to meet changing exigencies (e.g. differential population growth of interdependent strata), then it will be stable even if social dissent does develop. Conversely, if the social centre is inflexible and the stratification system correspondingly rigid, then emergent contradictions will precipitate a social revolution.

It should be clear that the Indian caste system approximates closely to a system with a dominant social centre. The strength of the Brahman castes is due to their combination of social with cultural power and in many cases with control over the agricultural economy. This system is none the less an imperfect example because of the malintegration between social and political power in the macrosocietal system; the emergence of independent economic centres with industrialisation and the British land settlements also contradicted the requirements of continued social dominance. Within the village community before British rule, however, political power was weak and insignificant and the social centre was the dominant force in village life. The leading castes were able to maintain their hegemony and to incorporate both powerful emergent interests and dissensual movements within the caste system as a whole. This hegemony combined with the limited economic exploitation to encourage the survival of the caste system largely unchanged for many generations.

A society with a *strong cultural centre* is also unlikely to be found in its pure form although an effective cultural system is a

141

necessary condition for the maintenance of an economic, political or social hegemony. Whereas dominant economic or political centres can resort to situational sanctions when confronted by non-compliance with economic or political commitments, dominant social or cultural centres can rely in the last resort only on intentional sanctions (i.e. shame and guilt respectively). None the less it is theoretically possible for the hegemony of a cultural centre to be so strong that political and economic centres can be invoked to sanction recalcitrant revolutionaries and, indeed, so strong that situational sanctions will be unnecessary owing to the intensity of central and peripheral commitments to the central cultural values. This seems most likely to happen where a religious or other charismatic movement has been routinised and thereby has facilitated the efficient mobilisation of non-cultural sanctions and resources.

A dominant cultural centre must therefore ensure that socialisation into the dominant values is adequate to the demands of institutional integration and society-wide consensus. In addition it has to insulate all members of the society from contact with values and beliefs that contradict the dominant value system and its assertions about the world. The dominant values themselves must be sufficiently flexible in their interpretation to allow for variation in the ability of the different power systems to produce their outputs without precipitating deprivation. In so far as the values are inflexible, then the cultural centre must also be able to regulate the output of these systems to coincide with the institutionalised expectations. In particular their operation must be regulated to avoid emergent contradictions that undermine the power of the cultural centre and also to avoid the emergence of marginal centres that articulate radical dissent and mobilise peripheral support against the cultural order. Finally, wherever dissent does develop, the dominant centre must be able to redirect it along institutionalised channels or repress it through the mobilisation of situational sanctions. While the dominant values must be sufficiently flexible to overcome the tendency for varia-tion in system outputs, control over the interpretation of these values must be firmly vested in the centre itself. Secularisation of the dominant value system is incompatible with the continued hegemony of the cultural centre and attempts to liberalise their interpretation must therefore be rigorously opposed. Provided all these conditions are met, then the dominant cultural centre will continue to be strong and efficient. However, increasing structural differentiation and technological complexity are bound to make such conditions more difficult to meet and thus eventually to cause a loss of cultural hegemony and the supercession of another power centre to dominance. This process can be seen in the gradual decline of the Catholic Church as a major secular as well as religious power during the Middle Ages and after the Reformation.

In outlining the conditions for the continued domination of different types of strong centre we have assumed throughout that the strong centre also controls an effective cultural system. In so far as this is untrue then social order and stability must depend on the lessening of exploitation and on the maintenance of a favourable balance of physical power on the part of the centres involved. We have already discussed the prerequisites of these two conditions in earlier chapters, and we have illustrated them in the present chapter.

Conclusions

We have now completed our analysis of social order, reform and revolution and also the presentation of our case studies. In the present chapter we provided illustrations from exploitative societies and ended with some further reflections on the conditions of social order and stability in differentiated societies. We turn now to a review of the arguments for and against the general model that has informed both the analysis and the case studies.

8 Retrospect and Prospect

We have now completed for the present our analysis of order, reform and revolution and in this concluding chapter we discuss the main arguments and problems involved in its presentation and development. It is obvious that much work remains to be done and we therefore also take the opportunity of outlining the main directions of theoretical and empirical inquiry that are necessary to the further development and evaluation of the present model. Finally, we reconsider the questions posed in the very first chapter regarding the sociological analysis of reform and revolution and the role of the sociologist in their promotion or prevention.

Retrospect

We have been concerned in this monograph with the development of a general symbolic model of social order, reform and revolution. Symbolic models are based on conceptual definition and interconnection and the articulation of this conceptual framework with rationally consistent assumptions in order to generate meaningful hypotheses. We first reviewed the three major contemporary sociological approaches to structural analysis and abstracted the main emergent themes and perspectives. Next, we presented the general analytical framework which provides the conceptual infrastructure for our more specific model of social order and stability. This conceptual structure was then articulated with a set of assumptions derived from empirical observation and theoretical argument. We have not yet attempted a formalised statement of the model nor have we presented an operational system from which to derive empirically testable propositions. Our case studies none the less necessarily imply several operational measures in illustrating different aspects of the general model. Formalisation and operationalisation must clearly be the next items on the theoretical and the empirical agenda respectively and only then will it be fruitful to return to an evaluation and reconstruction of the conceptual framework.

The rationale for the construction of our symbolic model derives from power, exchange and institutionalisation perspectives. For we believe that the dynamics of order, reform and revolution are codetermined by exchange and power relations and by the relative institutionalisation of the reactions to such relations. Power and exchange are equally important aspects of structural analysis and it is only a combination of their effects that yields a sound basis for sociological study and prediction. Thus a power potential may or may not be realised and it may be realised in an exploitative or even a beneficial manner; moreover, the nature of the exchange not only determines the reactions of the powerless to the exercise of power but also reacts back on the distribution of power itself. In this respect we have emphasised the importance of 'force activation' rather than 'basic force' assumptions about the nature of power relations. Whereas a 'basic force' model assumes that all actors exert all their power all the time, a 'force activation' model assumes that actors exert varying amounts of their full power potential and thus that there is a potential for co-operation as well as domination and opposition. Finally, the reaction to power and exchange relations may be more or less approved by those with power and this too has important effects on the dynamics of order, reform and revolution. Indeed we have distinguished between reform and revolution themselves in terms of the relative institutionalisation of the economic, political, social or cultural movements that effect such changes. Reform is thus a structural change that is approved by the powerful and revolution is a structural change that is derogated or proscribed by the powerful. Guided by this rationale we have attempted to develop a model that relates the various elements in a power-exchange relation to the dynamics of social order and disorder.

In separating the presentation of the general analytical framework and the articulation of the symbolic model we hope to have emphasised their relative independence of each other. Thus a need to reformulate our assumptions in the model, for example, need not detract from the utility of the more general conceptual framework. Conversely, similar assumptions could be articulated with an alternative analytical framework and, indeed, have been so articulated by other theorists. Likewise a less general investigation need not concern itself with the full range of variation in the analytical variables and can treat many of them as parameters – as we were forced by considerations of space to treat some of

145

the variables in our case studies. But this should not blind the investigator to the potential importance of their variation in other contexts. Similar arguments can be applied to the initial review of contemporary theories and to the concluding illustrations. For it is possible to evaluate the general analytical schema independently of its origins in the theoretical review and just as possible to consider the studies in order, reform and revolution apart from their connections with the symbolic model. Thus although the four main elements in this monograph are intended to form a unitary whole they can none the less be considered more or less independently. In the next section we do indeed consider some possible criticisms of these elements as well as pointing to some useful and some necessary areas of future work in this field.

Critical Appraisal

We have been concerned throughout this work with the development of a general model that combines the contributions of different sociological approaches to the analysis of order, reform and revolution. This very attempt is itself open to criticism on the grounds that the concern for continuity, codification, convergence and cumulation is in fact destructive of intellectual criticism and innovation.[1] But our concern is not just to show that the great theorists have come to a consensus unbeknown to themselves but also that each has neglected significant areas of inquiry considered by their opponents or has mentioned these areas only in an *ad hoc* or perfunctory fashion. We have been concerned not only with convergent themes but also with unilateral emphases that are none the less significant for sociological analysis. By providing a more general analytical framework within which the conflicts as well as the convergences between these theorists can be placed, we hope to have advanced rather than retarded criticism and innovation. Moreover, in so far as the present conceptual scheme can be articulated with different sets of assumptions to generate significantly different propositions, it is compatible with controversy as well as cumulation. While we hope to have developed a *general* model for the analysis of social order, reform and revolution, we did not intend it to be a *universal* model so omnicompetent in scope and application that all other models and approaches must be displaced and superseded. A pluralistic world requires a plurality of general theories as well as a plurality of middle-range and micro theories.

In the light of our professed concern with convergence there
146

is a second criticism that could perhaps be levelled against our work, namely, that we have tended to emphasise the contradictory and conflictual elements in social structure rather than the harmonious and non-conflictual. This is almost inevitable since the problem of order is inherent in all social relations – we qualify our statement advisably because so many theorists have felt able to ignore the elements of conflict in social life. Moreover, we have also emphasised the requirements of social order and stability in the development and amplification of our model – the need for reciprocity, consensus and institutional integration. Furthermore, it cannot be too often stressed that, in so far as a model of social order cannot explain the dynamics of disorder, then neither can it fully account for the origins and persistence of order itself. It was for this reason that we suggested the reformulation of functionalism in terms of the need to regulate power and exchange relations between concrete actors and between more abstract functional systems in order to maintain social order and stability. If this reformulation were adopted many of the empirical, as opposed to philosophical, problems involved in its application could be resolved.[2] Provided that it is balanced by recognition of the harmonious and non-conflictual elements, therefore, emphasis on conflict and contradiction is as essential to the understanding of order as it is for the understanding of disorder.

A further target of criticism in our general model can perhaps be found in its apparent 'type-atomism', that is, the specification of distinct types of society conducive to order and disorder rather than the presentation of a matrix or calculus that allows for continuous variation in the major independent and dependent variables. Unfortunately such an approach is impossible at the present stage of theoretical development in the model, and the formulation of causal models must be one of the next steps.[3] The tendency towards such 'type-atomism' is none the less counterbalanced both by the prior presentation of the analytical variables that are employed to define the different societal types and also by the more general statement of the causal principles and assumptions involved in their construction. Furthermore, we have often drawn our illustrations from mixed types of society and have also attempted to show the effects of social order and stability of variations through time in the major independent variables. Thus we have tried as far as possible to circumvent the tendencies to 'type-atomism' and hope eventually to overcome them completely.

The nature of our illustrations raises two further problems in the evaluation of the present model, namely, the value question and the issue of critical tests. As we pointed out in the discussion of the value problem, in so far as there is a gap between a theoretical concept and its operational measure, then even classification involves value judgement. This must be particularly true of our examples since the subsumption of any society under one of our 'types' is necessarily linked to negatively evaluated concepts such as inequality and exploitation. This problem is most acute for mixed examples such as Northern Ireland, the Indian caste system and the Third Reich. It is partly for this reason that operationalisation and especially quantitative operational definitions are so urgent for the future development of the model.

The illustrations also raise the problem of their adequacy to a rigorous non-experimental evaluation of the general model. We have emphasised throughout that the examples used in the presentation of the model are precisely *examples* and not critical tests. But it is clearly necessary to conduct several such tests if the model is to demonstrate its utility. We have already suggested two significant tests – a comparative analysis of the African kingdoms to examine the covariation between exploitation, inequality and social order; and a more detailed comparative examination of the Indian caste system. Dahrendorf implies several additional tests when he argues that conflict theories have failed to account adequately for the following: the absence of opposition in the Soviet Union, the emergence of fascism in Europe, the absence of socialism in the United States, and the end of ideology in contemporary Western capitalist societies. While Dahrendorf is incorrect in arguing that there is no opposition in the Soviet Union, it is true to say that opposition is largely uninstitutionalised; likewise the 'end of ideology' involves only the fragmentation of dissent and not the dissolution of ideological hegemony. None the less these are all important phenomena and they do provide four significant tests for any model of social order. We have already sketched more or less explicit explanations of the end of ideology and the emergence of fascism in terms of our own model; and the pattern of opposition in the Soviet Union and the absence of socialism in the United States can be explained in terms of their strong political and economic centres respectively. A rigorous evaluation of the model would need to examine these explanations in more detail and also

148

compare them with those offered by alternative theoretical frameworks. Finally, the scope of the model could be tested through its application to types of social movement that have so far been neglected in our concern with political and economic dissent.

The extension of the tests in this way would also meet another objection to the present model, that is, its inadequacy in the light of the criteria set out in our first chapter for identifying a 'good' theory. We argued that the greater the number of hypotheses generated by the model, the wider their implications, the more parsimonious their formulation and the more precise their predictions, then the stronger the theoretical model. We have clearly put forward a large number of propositions in these pages and we hope that they appear parsimonious in their formulation. These propositions are relatively imprecise in predictive power, however, owing to the previously-mentioned operational problems and to the theoretical problems posed by the irreducible element of voluntarism in human action. Moreover, the implications of these propositions have so far been 'tested' on only a limited range of cases. Accordingly the extension of the model to include, say, religious movements would greatly strengthen the case in its favour. In so far as religious movements are concerned with power – especially those forms of power that are not adequately comprehended (i.e. the 'supernatural') – and attempt to control such powers through various means, then they can easily be incorporated into the general model.[4] Likewise the model could be extended to include other types of movement that have been ignored to date in our analysis and examples.

Although the implications of the present model have not perhaps been extended as far as they might properly be spread, they are none the less quite wide in comparison with many other general theories. Orthodox Marxism is often described as the sociology of capitalism rather than of all structures and processes; yet it has still contributed much to the analysis of other types of society. In contrast, our own approach is concerned with no particular social formation but is hopefully more general in application. But this generality has clearly been obtained at the cost of neglecting the detailed operation of particular systems and types of society. Any future work must attempt to redress this imbalance through the accomplishment of two main tasks. Firstly, we must develop our theoretical understanding of the power and exchange processes that underly the operation of different power

149

systems and the specific character of inflationary, deflationary and equilibrating cycles in each system. Secondly, we must develop more specific models of particular types of society through more rigorous statement of the assumptions that articulate the general model. We have already attempted to specify the conditions for social order and stability in complex societies with different types of strong centre, for example, and we should now make similar attempts for other types of society. In this way it should prove possible to combine the best of both particular and general theoretical models of social order and social change.

Thus there is still much to be done before we can begin to claim that the new perspective presented in these pages is more than an initial step in the development of a fully formalised, fully operationalised theory. That a genuine synthesis of the different theoretical perspectives reviewed above is possible along these lines should now be apparent, however, and we hope that other sociologists will feel encouraged to develop this, or a similar, theoretical model. It is clear that the most immediate theoretical tasks lie precisely in the fields of formalisation and operationalisation so that the model can be subject to more adequate tests. The second major area of further work lies in the extension and refinement of the model as it applies to different power systems and different types of society. But we must now turn to answer the questions posed in our very first chapter and patient of reply for so long.

Conclusions

At the beginning of this work we quoted three very different views on the nature of the disorder in Northern Ireland and then asked a number of questions about the role of sociology in the interpretation and explanation of these views and the events with which they were concerned. It is a fundamental premiss of this monograph and, indeed, of all sociologies of revolution, that sociology can be useful in the attempt to understand these questions. The extent to which it can do so is not, of course, bound up with the particular merits or demerits of the present approach and should not be evaluated in these terms. However, to the extent that the reader believes that we have understood not only these views and events but also social order and disorder in general, then sociology as a whole can be vindicated.

We have argued that it is indeed possible to develop a general theory of order, reform and revolution and that this theory will demonstrate certain similarities between the conflicts in Northern Ireland and conflicts in comparable types of social system. We should not expect all instances of revolution to be alike in their origins, course and consequences; but we should be able to identify specific subtypes of reformist and revolutionary movement that are capable of generalisation.[5] A general theory of order, reform and revolution does not have to state a single, universal sequence of reform or revolution nor a single, universal cause of social order: but where a plurality of causes and sequences is suggested they must all be derived from the same set of assumptions applied to different contexts, otherwise the theory itself will be indeterminate. It is for this reason that the disorder in Northern Ireland is only comparable to disorder in societies of the same type, that is, those with strong politico-economic centres that exercise a partial hegemony over the periphery. The further one moves from this societal type, the less close will be the patterns of deprivation, dissent and disorder.

Although it is possible to develop a general theory that is able to describe the social factors that underly individual and collective dissent and that determine the relative success or failure of their attempts to reorganise the distribution of power and rewards, it is not possible for the theory to predict accurately the outcome of any given structural situation or any given movement. For there is an irreducible element of voluntarism in human action that interacts with the objective structural factors to produce a more or less broad range of possible outcomes. It is this element of voluntarism that inspires the Marxist emphasis on the unity of theory and practice in which positive actions are required to realise what is theoretically possible. Yet voluntarism is only one element in this unity: the other is theoretical understanding of objective conditions and the latter can exercise more or less severe constraints on human action. It is for this reason that we emphasised the importance of emergent contradictions in the development of radical change and the significance of the balance of power between contending forces. It is also for this reason that one must distinguish between social disorder and instability: a society can be subject to widespread disorder and still be stable owing to the balance of power and the effects of institutional inertia. Notwithstanding its contradictions and its conflicts, this is the case with Northern Ireland, where the centre remains strong and is supported by the British political and economic centres as well as many from the Protestant and the Catholic peripheries. Unless there is a radical intensification of its emergent contradictions and a loss of British support (or unless there is a radical lessening of exploitation) Northern Ireland will remain a stable but intermittently disorderly society.

It is the element of voluntarism and its concomitant theoretical indeterminism that provide both the freedom and the opportunity for the individual to intervene and change the course of events within the limits set by objective conditions. Whether or not successful, he is free to promote reciprocity rather than exploitation, liberty rather than repression, persuasion rather than coercion, social justice rather than injustice. This is both the right and the responsibility of the social scientist as much as any other individual.

Bibliography

The following list of books and articles is not intended to be an exhaustive guide to the vast literature on social order, reform and revolution; it is simply a list of the works cited in the presentation of our own perspective on these phenomena. Useful general bibliographies can be found in those books in the list that are preceded by an asterisk (*).

C. Ackerman and T. Parsons, 'The Concept of "Social System" as a Theoretical Device', in 'Concepts, Theory, and Explanation in the Behavioural Sciences', ed. G. J. DiRenzo (New York, Random House 1966) pp. 24–40.

H. Alavi, 'Peasants and Revolution', in 'Socialist Register 1965', ed. R. Miliband and J. Saville (London, Merlin Press 1965) pp. 241–77.

G. Almond and B. Powell, 'Comparative Politics' (Boston, Little Brown 1966).

L. Althusser, 'Contradiction and Overdetermination', in 'New Left Review', 41 (1967) 15–35.

P. Anderson, 'Origins of the Present Crisis', in 'Towards Socialism', ed. P. Anderson and R. Blackburn (London, Fontana 1965) pp. 11–52.

S. Andreski, 'Parasitism and Subversion' (London, Weidenfeld and Nicolson 1966).
   'Military Organisation and Society', 2nd ed. (London, Routledge 1968).

D. Apter, 'The Role of Traditionalism in the Political Modernisation of Ghana and Uganda', in 'World Politics', xii (1959) 45–68.

H. Arendt, 'On Revolution' (New York, Viking Press 1963).

S. Avinieri, 'Karl Marx : Social and Political Thought' (London, Cambridge University Press 1968).

F. G. Bailey, 'Closed Social Stratification in India', in 'European Journal of Sociology', iv (1963) 107–41.
   'Caste and the Economic Frontier' (London, OUP 1957).
   'Stratagems and Spoils' (Oxford, Blackwell 1969).

J. A. Banks, 'Marxist Sociology in Action' (London, Faber 1970).

153

O. Banks, 'The Sociology of Education' (London, Batsford 1968).

P. A. Baran and P. M. Sweezy, 'Monopoly Capital' (Harmondsworth, Penguin 1968).

D. P. Barritt and C. F. Carter, 'The Northern Ireland Problem' London, OUP 1962).

B. M. Barry, 'Political Argument' (London, Routledge 1965).
    'Sociologists, Economists, and Democracy' (London, Collier-Macmillan 1969).

J. Beattie, 'Checks on the Abuse of Political Power in Some African States', in 'Sociologus', ix (1959) 97–115.

H. Becker, 'Through Values to Social Interpretation' (Durham, N.C., Duke University Press 1950).

D. Bell (ed.), 'The Radical Right' (New York, Anchor 1964).

R. Bell, D. V. Edwards, and R. Wagner (eds.), 'Political Power' (New York, Free Press 1969).

R. N. Bellah, 'Religious Aspects of Modernisation in Turkey and Japan', in 'American Journal of Sociology', xliv (1958) 1–5.

C. S. Belshaw, 'Traditional Markets and Modern Exchange' (Englewood Cliffs, Prentice-Hall 1965).

P. M. Berger (ed.), 'Marxism and Sociology' (New York, Macmillan 1968).

P. M. Berger and T. Luckmann, 'The Social Construction of Reality' (London, Allen Lane 1967).

P. van den Berghe, 'Dialectic and Functionalism', in 'American Sociological Review', xxviii (1963) 695–705.

M. Bernal, 'China' (mimeo, King's College, Cambridge 1969).

G. D. Berreman, 'Caste in India and the United States', in 'American Journal of Sociology', lxvi (1960) 120–7.

E. Bittner, 'Radicalism and the Organisation of Radical Movements', in 'American Sociological Review', xxviii (1963) 928–40.

M. Black (ed.) 'The Social Theories of Talcott Parsons' (Englewood Cliffs, Prentice-Hall 1961).

P. M. Blau, 'Some Critical Remarks on Weber's Theory of Authority', in 'American Political Science Review', lvii (1963) 305–16.
    'Exchange and Power in Social Life' (New York, Wiley 1964).

S. Box and J. Forde, 'Some Questionable Assumptions in the Theory of Status Inconsistency', in 'Sociological Review', xvii (1969) 191–8.

H. C. Bredemeier and R. M. Stephenson, 'The Analysis of Social Systems' (New York, Holt Reinhart & Winston 1962).

*C. Brinton, 'The Anatomy of Revolution', 2nd ed. (New York, Anchor 1957).

K. Burridge, 'New Heaven, New Earth' (Oxford, Blackwell 1969).

*P. Calvert, 'Revolution' (London, Macmillan 1970).

J. M. Cammett, 'Antonio Gramsci and the Origins of Italian Communism' (Stanford, Stanford University Press 1967).

S. Carmichael and C. V. Hamilton, 'Black Power' (Harmondsworth, Penguin 1969).

J. Ch'en, 'Mao and the Chinese Revolution' (London, OUP 1965).

V. G. Childe, 'What Happened in History' (Harmondsworth, Penguin 1964).

K. Chorley, 'Armies and the Art of Revolution' (London, Faber 1943).

P. Cohen, 'Modern Social Theory' (London, Heinemann 1968).

L. F. Coser, 'The Functions of Social Conflict' (New York, Free Press 1956).

R. L. Curry and L. L. Wade, 'A Theory of Political Exchange' (Englewood Cliffs, Prentice-Hall 1968).

R. A. Dahl, 'The Concept of Power', in 'Behavioural Scientist', ii (1957) 201–15.

   (ed.), 'Political Oppositions in Western Democracies' (New Haven, Yale University Press 1966).

R. Dahrendorf, 'Toward a Theory of Social Conflict', in 'Journal of Conflict Resolution', ii (1958) 170–83.

   'Class and Class Conflict in Industrial Society' (London, Routledge 1959).

   'Conflict After Class' (London, Longmans 1967).

   'Essays in the Theory of Society' (London, Routledge 1968).

   'Society and Democracy in Germany' (London, Weidenfeld & Nicolson 1968).

R. Debray, 'Revolution in the Revolution?' (Harmondsworth, Penguin 1968).

L. de Paor, 'Divided Ulster' (Harmondsworth, Penguin 1970).

R. Desai, 'The Social Background of Indian Nationalism' (Bombay, Popular Prakashan 1948).

K. W. Deutsch, 'The Nerves of Government' (New York, Free Press 1963).

B. Devlin, 'The Price of My Soul' (London, Pan 1969).

'Disturbances in Northern Ireland : Report of the Commission Appointed by the Governor of N. Ireland' (Belfast 1969).

R. Dubin, 'Theory Building' (New York, Free Press 1969).

H. Dumont, 'Homo Hierarchicus' (London, Weidenfeld & Nicolson 1970).

D. Easton, 'Political Anthropology', in 'Biennial Review of Anthropology', ed. H. Siegel (Stanford, Stanford University Press 1959) pp. 210–262.

H. Eckstein (ed.) 'Internal War' (New York, Free Press 1964).

L. P. Edwards, 'The Natural History of Revolution' (Chicago, University of Chicago Press 1927).

O. D. Edwards, 'The Sins of Our Fathers' (Dublin, Gill & Macmillan 1970).

S. N. Eisenstadt, 'Internal Contradictions in Bureaucratic Empires', in 'Comparative Studies in Society and History', i (1958) 58–75.

'Primitive Political Systems', in 'American Anthropologist', lxi (1959) 200–20.

'Religious Organisations and Political Process in Centralised Empires', in 'Journal of Asian Studies', xxi (1962) 271–94.

'Political Systems of Empires' (New York, Free Press 1963).

'Institutionalisation and Change', in 'American Sociological Review', xxix (1964) 49–59.

'Prestige, Participation, and Strata-Formation', in 'Social Stratification', ed. J. A. Jackson (London, CUP 1968) pp. 62–103.

F. Engels, 'Origins of the Family, Private Property, and the State' (New York, International Publishers 1942).

A. Etzioni, 'A Comparative Analysis of Complex Organisations' (New York, Free Press 1961).

E. E. Evans-Pritchard, 'The Nuer' (Oxford, Clarendon Press 1940).

E. E. Evans-Pritchard and M. Fortes (eds.), 'African Political Systems' (London, OUP 1940).

E. Eyck, 'A History of the Weimar Republic', 2 vols. (London, OUP 1962–4).

J. K. Fairbank, 'The United States and China' (Cambridge, Mass., Harvard UP 1959).

L. A. Fallers, 'Despotism, Status Culture, and Social Mobility in an African Kingdom', in 'Comparative Studies in Society and History', ii (1959) 11–32.

S. F. Finer, 'The Man on Horseback' (London, Pall Mall 1962).

C. P. Fitzgerald, 'The Birth of Communist China' (Harmondsworth, Penguin 1964).

M. Fortes, 'The Dynamics of Clanship among the Tallensi' (London, OUP 1945).
  'The Structure of Unilineal Descent Groups', in 'American Anthropologist', lv (1953) 17–41.

G. M. Foster, 'Peasant Society and the Image of Limited Good', in 'American Anthropologist', lxii (1965) 293–315.

M. Freilich, 'Toward a Model of Social Structure', in 'Journal of the Royal Anthropological Institute', xciv (1964) 183–200.

R. W. Friedrichs, 'A Sociology of Sociology' (New York, Free Press 1970).

J. A. Galtung, 'A Structural Theory of Aggression', in 'Journal of Peace Research', i (1965) 95–119.

P. Gibbon, 'The Dialectic of Religion and Class in Ulster', in 'New Left Review', 55 (1970) 20–41.

A. Giddens, 'Power in the Recent Writings of Talcott Parsons', in 'Sociology', ii (1968) 256–72.

C. Y. Glock and R. Stark, 'Religion and Society in Tension' (Chicago, Rand McNally 1965).

M. Gluckman, 'Custom and Conflict in Africa' (Oxford, Blackwell 1956).
  'Politics, Law, and Ritual in Tribal Society' (Oxford, Blackwell 1965).

M. Godelier, 'System, Structure, and Contradiction in "Capital"', in 'Socialist Register 1967', ed. R. Miliband and J. Saville (London, Merlin Press 1967) pp. 91–119.

I. W. Goffman, 'Status Inconsistency and Preference for Change in Power', in 'American Sociological Review', xxii (1957) 275–81.

W. J. Goode, 'A Theory of Role Strain', in 'American Sociological Review', xxv (1960) 483–96.

J. Goody, 'Technology, Tradition, and the African State' (London, OUP 1971).

A. W. Gouldner, 'The Norm of Reciprocity', in 'American Sociological Review', xxv (1960) 161–78.
  'The Coming Crisis of Western Sociology' (London, Heinemann 1971).

A. Gramsci, 'The Modern Prince and Other Essays' (New York, International Publishers 1969).

N. Gross et al., 'Explorations in Role Analysis' (New York, Wiley 1958).

157

*T. R. Gurr, 'Why Men Rebel' (Princeton, PUP 1970).

J. R. Gusfield (ed.) 'Protest, Reform, and Revolt' (New York, Wiley 1970).

I. Hamilton, 'The Irish Tangle', in 'Conflict Studies', 6 (1970).

N. Harris, 'Beliefs and Society' (London, Watts 1968).

J. P. Harrison, 'The Communists and Chinese Peasant Rebellions' (London, Gollancz 1969).

E. J. Hobsbawm, 'Primitive Rebels' (Manchester, Manchester University Press 1959).

R. Hofheinz, 'The Ecology of Chinese Communist Success', in 'Chinese Communist Politics in Action', ed. A. D. Barnett (Seattle, University of Washington Press 1969) pp. 3–77.

G. C. Homans, 'Social Behaviour: its elementary forms' (London, Routledge 1962).

I. L. Horowitz, 'Consensus, Conflict, and Co-operation', in 'Social Forces', xli (1962) 177–88.

R. A. Humphreys, 'Latin America: the caudillo tradition', in 'Soldiers and Governments', ed. M. Howard (London, Eyre and Spottiswoode 1959).

S. P. Huntington (ed.), 'Changing Patterns of Military Politics' (New York, Free Press 1962).

'Political Order in Changing Societies' (New Haven, Yale University Press 1968).

G. Ionescu, 'The Politics of the European Communist States' (London, Weidenfeld & Nicolson 1968).

M. Janowitz, 'The Military in the Political Development of the New States' (Chicago, University of Chicago Press 1964).

R. D. Jessop, 'Exchange and Power in Structural Analysis', in 'Sociological Review', xxvii (1969) 415–437.

'Civility and Traditionalism in English Political Culture', in 'British Journal of Political Science', 1 (1971) 1–24.

C. J. Johnson, 'Peasant Nationalism and Communist Power' (Stanford, Stanford University Press 1962).

'Revolution and the Social System' (Stanford, Hoover Institute 1964).

'Revolutionary Change' (London, University of London Press 1969).

M. Kalab, 'The Specificity of the Marxist Conception of Sociology', in 'Marxism and Sociology', ed. P. M. Berger (New York, Macmillan 1968) pp. 58–76.

D. Katz and E. Stotland, 'A Preliminary Statement to a Theory of Attitude Change', in 'Psychology', ed. S. Koch (New York, McGraw-Hill 1959) iii pp. 243–76.

L. M. Killian, 'The Impossible Revolution' (New York, Random House 1968).

M. Kling, 'Violence and Politics in Latin America', in 'Sociological Review Monographs', 11 (1967) 119–32.

P. M. Kolenda, 'Toward a Model of the Hindu "Jajmani" System', in 'Human Organisation', xxii (1963) 11–31.

L. Krader, 'The Emergence of the State' (Englewood Cliffs, Prentice-Hall 1968).

H. D. Lasswell et al., 'World Revolutionary Elites' (Cambridge, Mass., M.I.T. Press 1965).

E. R. Leach (ed.), 'Aspects of Caste in South India, Ceylon, and North-west Pakistan' (London, CUP 1960).

*C. Leiden and K. M. Schmidt, 'The Politics of Violence' (Englewood Cliffs, Prentice-Hall 1967).

E. M. Lemert, 'Human Deviance, Social Problems, and Social Control' (Englewood Cliffs, Prentice-Hall 1967).

V. I. Lenin, 'The State and Revolution', in 'The Essential Left' (London, Allen & Unwin 1960).
    'What is to be Done?' (Panther edition, London, 1970).

G. E. Lenski, 'Power and Privilege' (New York, McGraw-Hill 1966).

D. E. Lerner, 'Some Comments on Center-Periphery Relations', in 'Comparing Nations', ed. R. L. Merritt and S. Rokkan (New Haven, Yale UP 1968), pp. 259–65.

G. Lichtheim, 'Marx and the Asiatic Mode of Production', in 'St. Antony's Papers', xiv (1963) 86–112.
    'Marxism' (London, Routledge 1964).

S. M. Lipset, 'Political Man' (London, Heinemann 1959).

S. M. Lipset and S. Rokkan (eds.), 'Party Systems and Voter Alignments' (New York, Free Press 1968).

D. Lockwood, 'Some Remarks on the "Social System"', in 'British Journal of Sociology', vii (1956) 134–46.
    'Social Integration and System Integration', in 'Explorations in Social Change', ed. G. K. Zollschan and W. Hirsch (London, Routledge 1964) pp. 244–56.
    'Sources of Variation in Working-Class Images of Society', in 'Sociological Review', xiv (1966) 49–267.

J. R. Lucas, 'The Principles of Politics' (Oxford, Clarendon Press 1966).

E. Luttwak, 'Coup d'Etat' (London, Allen Lane 1968).

F. Machlup, 'Another View of Cost-Push and Demand-Pull Inflation', in 'Review of Economics and Statistics', lxii (1960) 125–39.

L. Mair, 'Primitive Government' (Harmondsworth, Penguin 1962).

M. Mann, 'The Social Cohesion of Liberal Democracy', in 'American Sociological Review', xxx (1970) 423–39.

H. Marcuse, 'One-Dimensional Man' (Sphere edition, 1968).

H. Marcuse et al., 'A Critique of Pure Tolerance' (London, Cape 1969).

K. Marx, 'A Contribution to the Critique of Political Economy' (Chicago, University of Chicago Press 1904).

'Early Writings', ed. T. B. Bottomore (London, Watts 1963).

'Capital' (London, Lawrence & Wishart 1962).

K. Marx and F. Engels, 'The Communist Manifesto' (London, Allen & Unwin 1948).

'The Holy Family' (Moscow, Foreign Languages Publishing House, 1956).

'The German Ideology' (New York, International Publishers 1967).

'On Britain' (London, Lawrence & Wishart 1962).

'Selected Correspondence' (Moscow, Foreign Languages Publishing House 1962).

D. Matza, 'Becoming Deviant' (Englewood Cliffs, Prentice-Hall 1969).

J. A. Merrington, 'Theory and Practice in Gramsci's Marxism', in 'Socialist Register 1968', ed. R. Miliband and J. Saville (London, Merlin Press 1968) pp. 145–76.

R. Michels, 'Political Parties' (Dover edition, New York 1959).

J. Middleton and D. Tait (eds.), 'Tribes Without Rulers' (London, Routledge 1958).

R. Miliband, 'Marx and the State', in 'Socialist Register 1965', ed. R. Miliband and J. Saville (London, Merlin Press 1965) pp. 278–96.

'The State in Capitalist Society' (London, Weidenfeld & Nicolson 1969).

C. W. Mills, 'The Power Elite' (New York, OUP 1956).

'The Marxists' (Harmondsworth, Penguin 1963).

'The Sociological Imagination' (Harmondsworth, Penguin 1970).

W. C. Mitchell, 'Sociological Analysis and Politics' (Englewood Cliffs, Prentice-Hall 1967).

'The Shape of Political Theory to Come: from Political Sociology to Political Economy', in 'American Behavioural Scientist', xi (1967) 8–37.

B. Moore, 'Social Origins of Dictatorship and Democracy' (London, Allen Lane 1967).

S. F. Nadel, 'A Black Byzantium' (London, OUP 1940).

'The Theory of Social Structure' (London, Cohen & West 1957).

E. Nagel, 'The Structure of Science' (London, Routledge 1961).

P. Nettl and R. Robertson, 'International Systems and the Modernisation of Societies' (London, Faber 1967).

F. Neumann, 'Behemoth' (London, OUP 1944).

T. Nichols, 'Ownership, Control, and Ideology' (London, Allen & Unwin 1969).

E. Nolte, 'Three Faces of Fascism' (London, Weidenfeld & Nicolson 1967).

E. A. Nordlinger, 'The Working Class Tories' (London, Mac-Gibbon & Kee 1967).

M. Olsen, 'The Logic of Collective Action' (Cambridge, Mass., Harvard UP 1965).

K. F. Otterbein, 'Internal Wars; a cross-cultural study', in 'American Anthropologist', lxx (1968) 277–89.

K. F. Otterbein and S. C. Otterbein, 'An Eye for an Eye, a Tooth for a Tooth', in 'American Anthropologist', lxvii (1965) 1470–82.

F. Parkin, 'Middle Class Radicalism' (Manchester, Manchester University Press 1968).

G. Parry, 'Political Elites' (London, Allen & Unwin 1969).

T. Parsons, 'The Structure of Social Action' (New York, Free Press 1937).

'The Social System' (London, Routledge 1951).

'Essays in Sociological Theory' (New York, Free Press 1956).

'Structure and Process in Modern Societies' (New York, Free Press, 1960).

'Pattern Variables Revisited', in 'American Sociological Review', xxv (1960) 467–83.

'Some Considerations on the Theory of Social Change', in 'Rural Sociology', xxvi (1961) 219–39.

'Societies' (Englewood Cliffs, Prentice-Hall 1967).

'Sociological Theory and Modern Society' (New York, Free Press 1967).

161

'On the Concept of Value Commitments' in 'Sociological Inquiry', xxxviii (1968).

'Systems Analysis: Social Systems', in 'International Encyclopedia of Social Sciences', ed. R. Sills (New York, Free Press 1968).

'Some Problems of General Theory', in 'Theoretical Socio- ed. J. C. McKinney and E. C. Tyriakian (New York, Appleton Century Crofts 1970) pp. 26–68.

T. Parsons and E. A. Shils (eds.) 'Towards a General Theory of Action' (New York, Harper 1962).

T. Parsons et al., 'Theories of Society' (New York, Free Press 1961).

T. Parsons and N. J. Smelser, 'Economy and Society' (London, Routledge 1956).

T. Parsons and W. R. White, 'The Link Between Character and Society', in 'Culture and Social Character', ed. S. M. Lipset and L. Lowenthal (New York, Free Press 1961) pp. 89–135.

J. Pen, 'Harmony and Conflict in Modern Society' (London, McGraw-Hill 1966).

K. Polanyi et al., 'Trade and Market in the Early Empires' (New York, Free Press 1957).

'Police in Northern Ireland: Report of a Commission Appointed by the Governor of Northern Ireland' (Belfast, 1969).

C. Posner (ed.) 'Reflections on the Revolution in France 1968' (Harmondsworth, Penguin 1969).

O. Ramsoy, 'Social Groups as System and Subsystem' (New York, Free Press 1963).

J. Rawls, 'Distributive Justice', in 'Politics, Philosophy, and Society', ed. P. Laslett and W. G. Runciman (Oxford, Blackwell 1967) iii, pp. 58–82.

J. A. Rex, 'Key Problems in Sociological Theory' (London, Routledge 1961).

J. Robinson, 'Piero Sraffa and the Rate of Exploitation', in 'New Left Review', xxxi (1965) 28–34.

M. P. Rogin, 'The Intellectuals and McCarthy' (Cambridge, Mass., MIT 1967).

G. Roth, 'The Social Democrats in Imperial Germany' (Englewood Cliffs, Prentice-Hall 1965).

H. Rothfels, 'German Opposition to Hitler' (Chicago, University of Chicago Press 1962).

R. S. Rudner, 'Philosophy of Social Science' (Englewood Cliffs, Prentice-Hall 1966).

L. I. Rudolph and S. H. Rudolph, 'The Political Role of India's Caste Associations', in 'Pacific Affairs', xxxiii (1960) 5–22.

W. G. Runciman, 'Relative Deprivation and Social Justice' (London, Routledge 1966).

    'Justice, Congruence, and Professor Homans', in 'European Journal of Sociology', vii (1967) 115–28.

M. Sahlins, 'On the Sociology of Primitive Exchange', in 'The Relevance of Models to Social Anthropology', ed. M. Banton (London, Tavistock 1967) pp. 139–236.

I. Schapera, 'Government and Politics in Tribal Societies' (London, Watts 1956).

D. Schoenbaum, 'Hitler's Social Revolution' (London, Weidenfeld & Nicolson 1967).

F. Schurman and O. Schell (eds.), 'China Readings' (Harmondsworth, Penguin 1968).

M. B. Scott, 'The Social Sources of Alienation', in 'The New Sociology', ed. I. L. Horowitz (New York, OUP 1964) pp. 239–52.

P. Seale and M. McConville, 'French Revolution 1968' (Harmondsworth, Penguin 1968).

J. R. Seeley, 'Some Probative Problems in Social Science', in 'Sociology on Trial', ed. M. Stein and A. Vidich (Englewood Cliffs, Prentice-Hall 1963) pp. 53–65.

P. Selznick, 'T.V.A. and the Grass Roots' (Berkeley, University of California Press, 1953).

E. R. Service, 'The Hunters' (Englewood Cliffs, Prentice-Hall 1966).

E. A. Shils, 'Centre and Periphery', in 'The Logic of Personal Knowledge', ed. M. Polanyi (London, Routledge 1961) pp. 117–30.

L. Sklar, 'Moral Progress and Social Theory', in 'Ethics', lxxix (1969) 229–34.

N. J. Smelser, 'A Comparative View of Exchange Systems', in 'Economic Development and Cultural Change', vii (1959) 173–82.

    'Social Change and the Industrial Revolution' (London, Routledge 1959).

*   'Theory of Collective Behaviour' (London, Routledge 1962).

    'Essays in Sociological Explanation' (Englewood Cliffs, Prentice-Hall 1968).

M. G. Smith, 'On Segmentary Lineage Systems', in 'Journal of the Royal Anthropological Institute', lxxxvi (1956) 39–80.

'Pre-Industrial Stratification Systems', in 'Social Structure and Mobility in Economic Development', ed. N. J. Smelser and S. M. Lipset (London, Routledge 1966) pp. 141–76.

E. Snow, 'Red Star Over China' (London, Gollancz 1938).

A. W. Southall, 'Alur Society' (Cambridge, Heffer 1956).

P. Sraffa, 'The Production of Commodities by Commodities' (London, Cup 1963).

M. N. Srinivas, 'A Note on Sanskritisation and Westernisation', in 'Far Eastern Quarterly', xv (1955) 492–6.

A. S. Stinchcombe, 'Constructing Social Theory' (New York, Holt Reinhart Winston 1968).

*L. Stone, 'Theories of Revolution', in 'World Politics', xviii (1966) 159–76.

H. Stretton, 'The Political Sciences' (London, Routledge 1969).

R. Tanter and M. Midlarsky, 'A Theory of Revolution', in 'Journal of Conflict Resolution', xi (1967).

R. H. Tawney, 'Land and Labour in China' (London, Allen & Unwin 1932).

C. Taylor, 'Neutrality in Political Science', in 'Politics, Philosophy, and Society', ed. P. Laslett and W. G. Runciman (Oxford, Blackwell 1967) iii, pp. 25–57.

J. W. Thibaut and H. H. Kelley, 'The Social Psychology of Groups' (New York, Wiley 1959).

L. Trotsky, 'The Russian Revolution' (Anchor edition, New York 1959).

R. H. Turner, 'Sponsored and Contest Mobility in the School System', in 'American Sociological Review', xxv (1960) 855–67.

T. S. Terence, 'Parsons' Concept of "Generalised Media of Social Interaction" and its Relevance for Social Anthropology', in 'Sociological Inquiry', xxxviii (1968) 121–34.

C. A. Valentine, 'Culture and Poverty' (Chicago, University of Chicago Press 1968).

J. A. Van Doorn, 'Conflict in Formal Organisations', in 'Conflict in Society', ed. J. de Rueck and H. Knight (London, Churchill 1964) pp. 107–32.

(ed.), 'Military and Society' (The Hague, Moulton & Co. 1970).

H. R. Wagner, 'The Displacement of Scope' in 'The American Journal of Sociology', lxix (1963) 571–84.

W. L. Wallace, 'Sociological Theory' (London, Heinemann 1969).

E. V. Walter, 'Terror and Resistance' (New York, OUP 1969).

M. Weber, 'Charisma and Institution-Building', ed. S. N. Eisenstadt (Chicago, University of Chicago Press 1968).

G. A. Willer, 'Scientific Sociology' (Englewood Cliffs, Prentice-Hall 1966).

G. A. Williams, 'The Concept of "Egemonia" in the Thought of Gramsci', in 'Journal of the History of Ideas', xxi (1960) 586–99.

R. Williams, 'Communications' (Harmondsworth, Penguin 1968).

K. A. Wittfogel, 'Oriental Despotism' (New Haven, Yale UP 1952).

S. J. Woolf (ed.) 'European Fascism' (London, Weidenfeld & Nicolson 1968).

  (ed.) 'The Nature of Fascism' (London, Weidenfeld & Nicolson 1968).

P. M. Worsley, 'The Trumpet Shall Sound', 2nd ed. (London, Paladin 1970).

J. M. Yinger, 'Subculture and Contraculture', in 'American Sociological Review', xxv (1960) 625–35.

Notes

1 The Problem of Order

1. Captain Terence O'Neill, Prime Minister of Northern Ireland, television broadcast on B.B.C. and I.T.A. Networks, 9 Dec. 1968.
2. Bernadette Devlin, 'The Price of My Soul' (London, 1969) pp. 120 and 206.
3. Ian Paisley, speech as Chairman of the Ulster Constitution Defence Committee, 7 Oct. 1968.
4. 'Protestant Telegraph' (Belfast, 28 Dec. 1968) p. 8.
5. Cf. R. S. Rudner, 'Philosophy of Social Science' (Englewood Cliffs, 1966) p. 10; A. Stinchcombe, 'Constructing Social Theory' (New York, 1968) pp. 16–32; E. Nagel, 'The Structure of Science' (London, 1961) pp. 90–7.
6. Cf. N. J. Smelser, 'Essays in Sociological Explanation' (Englewood Cliffs, 1968) pp. 57–8; G. Willer, 'Scientific Sociology' (Englewood Cliffs, 1966) pp. 9–21.
7. Cf. Stinchcombe, 'Constructing Social Theory', pp. 17–22; and Rudner, 'Philosophy of Social Science', pp. 40–53.
8. Cf. Willer, 'Scientific Sociology', pp. 23–66. The three rationales are termed analogue, iconic and symbolic; and Willer prefers the symbolic approach to theory construction.
9. It is inadmissible, for example, to assume both that men desire power and that men do not desire power; one or other assumption will provide determinate predictions but not both conjointly.
10. Cf. R. Dubin, 'Theory Building' (New York, 1969) pp. 18–23.
11. Analogy is excluded because it is so rarely used: even Brinton's analogy from fever pathology is strongly influenced by abstraction and an emphasis on uniformities.
12. Cf. Eckstein's 'Introduction' to his 'Internal War' on the importance of careful definition of the theoretical universe: H. H. Eckstein (ed.), 'Internal War' (New York, 1964) pp. 8–16.
13. L. Stone, 'Theories of Revolution', in 'World Politics', xviii (1966) 159–76 (quotation from p. 164).
14. Ibid.; for further illustration and criticism, see A. Cobban, 'The Social Interpretation of the French Revolution' (London, 1964) and C. Tilly, 'The Analysis of a Counter-Revolution', in 'History and Theory', iii (1963) 30–58.
15. Cf. G. Lenski, 'Power and Privilege' (New York, 1966) pp. 17–22, on synthesis in theories of stratification; Lenski mentions two techniques – disaggregation of compounds and transformation of categorical concepts into variables.
16. The otherwise excellent confrontation between consensus and conflict theories presented by Mann is thus forced to admit a need for synthesis without suggesting how this may be achieved: see M. Mann, 'The Social Cohesion of Liberal Democracy', in 'American Sociological Review', xxxv (1970) 423–39.
17. Cf. T. Gurr, 'Why Men Rebel' (Princeton, 1970) pp. 16–8.
18. J. R. Lucas has shown that coercive sanctions are necessary for social

166

order in any society in which there is incomplete unselfishness, fallible judgement, imperfect information and incomplete control over membership: see 'The Principles of Politics' (Oxford, 1966) pp. 58–60. And E. V. Walter has demonstrated that at least some societies continually employ violence as a first resort with the full support of their members: see his 'Terror and Resistance' (New York, 1969) passim.

19. Cf. A Etzioni, 'A Comparative Analysis of Complex Organisations' (New York, 1961); Etzioni shows that coercion and remuneration are effective means of maintaining order in organisations where participants are alienative or calculative in outlook; normative control may be ineffective in such a situation – see pp. 12–14 and passim.

20. See, for example, S. P. Huntington, 'Political Order in Changing Societies' (New Haven, 1968) p. 264; C. Johnson, 'Revolution and the Social System' (Stanford, 1964) p. 4; H. Arendt, 'On Revolution' (New York, 1963) pp. 13–52 and especially 27–8.

21. See, for example, H. Eckstein (ed.), 'Internal War', p. 1 n; R. Tanter and M. Midlarsky, 'A Theory of Revolution', in 'Journal of Conflict Resolution', xi (1967) 265; R. A. Humphreys, 'Latin America: the Caudillo Tradition', in 'Soldiers and Governments', ed. M. Howard (London, 1959) p. 153; P. Calvert, 'Revolution' (London, 1970) p. 141.

22. See, for example, C. Brinton, 'Anatomy of Revolution' (Anchor Edition, New York, 1957) p. 4.

23. The *coup d'état*, for example, is supposedly institutionalised in Latin America: see M. Kling, 'Violence and Politics in Latin America', 'Sociological Review Monograph' 11 (1967) 119–32.

24. Cf. R. N. Bellah, 'Religious Aspects of Modernisation in Turkey and Japan', in 'American Journal of Sociology', xliv (1958) 1–5, on the question of admissibility as it affects attempts at modernisation.

25. The classic study of such processes is R. Michels, 'Political Parties' (New York, 1959 ed.); an interesting study of goal displacement in a reform movement is P. Selznick, 'TVA and the Grass Roots' (Berkeley, 1953). E. Bittner, 'Radicalism and the Organisation of Radical Movements', in 'American Sociological Review', xxviii (1963) 928–40, discusses solutions to these problems.

26. For a detailed discussion, see N. J. Smelser, 'Theory of Collective Behaviour' (London, 1962) pp. 319–33. On the importance of derogation in confirming a deviant role, see E. M. Lemert, 'Human Deviance, Social Problems, and Social Control' (Englewood Cliffs, 1967) pp. 40–60, and D. Matza, 'Becoming Deviant' (Englewood Cliffs, 1969) pp. 143–97.

27. Government vacillation is an often-cited characteristic of pre-revolutionary situations: see, for example, Brinton, 'Anatomy', pp. 265–67; C. J. Johnson, 'Revolutionary Change' (London, 1969 ed.) pp. 94–8; C. Leiden and K. M. Schmidt, 'The Politics of Violence' (Englewood Cliffs, 1968) pp. 46–52.

28. See, for example, K. Chorley, 'Armies and the Art of Revolution' (London, 1943); Huntington, 'Political Order', pp. 192–262; Gurr, 'Why Men Rebel', pp. 274–309; E. Luttwak, 'Coup D'Etat' (London, 1968); M. Janowitz, 'The Military in the Political Development of the New States' (Chicago, 1964); S. E. Finer, 'The Man on Horseback' (London, 1962).

29. Cf. R. Dahrendorf, 'Essays in the Theory of Society' (London, 1968) pp. 6–8. Dahrendorf argues that the choice of subject is irrelevant to the validity of research but suggests that 'the quality of scientific research improves to the extent that the choice of subject betrays a personal commitment on the part of the researcher' (ibid., p. 8).

167

30. Ibid., pp. 8–11; Rudner, 'Philosophy of Social Science', pp. 73–84.
31. Cf. H. Stretton, 'The Political Sciences' (London, 1969) pp. 161–95; J. Seeley, 'Some Probative Problems in Social Science', in 'Sociology on Trial', ed. M. Stein and A. Vidich (Englewood Cliffs, 1963) pp. 53–65; and C. Taylor, 'Neutrality in Political Science', in 'Politics, Philosophy, and Society', vol. 3, ed. P. Laslett and W. G. Runciman (Oxford, 1967) pp. 25–57.
32. Cf. Willer, 'Scientific Sociology', pp. 83–96.
33. This involves not only the inverse relation between the probability of rejecting a true hypothesis as false and that of accepting a false hypothesis as true, but also the possibility of conscious manipulation of criteria of acceptance to favour one's own theory.
34. See particularly Taylor in 'Politics, Philosophy, and Society', vol. 3 pp. 30–47.
35. Cf. Dahrendorf, 'Essays', p. 13; Dahrendorf also includes the presentation of untestable propositions as scientific under the rubric of ideological distortion.
36. Ibid., p. 14.
37. Cf. L. Sklar, 'Moral Progress and Social Theory', in 'Ethics', lxxix (1969) 229–34.
38. The distinction between undermining and overriding a value-position is drawn by Taylor in 'Politics, Philosophy, and Society', vol. 3 p. 38.
39. Sklar, in 'Ethics', p. 232; cf. W. G. Runciman, 'Relative Deprivation and Social Justice' London, 1966): 'a modified version of the contractual theory of justice can demonstrate in principle what kinds of grievances could be vindicated as legitimate and what reference group choices could therefore be described as "correct" ' (p. 248).
40. Sklar argues that his position does not reflect a value-judgement since only the perverse would override it: in 'Ethics', lxxix 232.
41. J. Rawls, 'Distributive Justice', in 'Philosophy, Politics, and Society', vol. 3, ed. P. Laslett and W. G. Runciman, pp. 58–82 at p. 61.
42. Runciman, 'Relative Deprivation', p. 264.
43. Ibid., p. 275.
44. Rawls in 'Politics, Philosophy, and Society', vol. 3 p. 78; distributive justice is defined in terms of procedures for reaching given distributions rather than in terms of the distributions themselves considered in isolation.
45. Cf. Dahrendorf, 'Essays', pp. 17–8.

2   Approaches to the Study of Order

1. The major contemporary exponents of the normative functionalist approach are Talcott Parsons and Neil Smelser. Their most important works include: T. Parsons, 'The Social System' (London, 1951); 'Essays in Sociological Theory' (New York, 1956); 'Structure and Process in Modern Societies' (New York, 1960); 'Sociological Theory and Modern Society' (New York, 1967); N. J. Smelser, 'Social Change and the Industrial Revolution' (London, 1959); 'Theory of Collective Behaviour' (London, 1962); 'Essays in Sociological Explanation' (Englewood Cliffs, 1968); and T. Parsons and N. J. Smelser, 'Economy and Society' (London, 1956). For a comprehensive bibliography of works by Parsons and of those by other normative functionalists, see W. C. Mitchell, 'Sociological Analysis and Politics' (Englewood Cliffs, 1967) pp. 193–208.
2. Parsons and Shils have defined social order as 'peaceful coexistence under conditions of scarcity'; this definition is the basis of our own

formulation. See T. Parsons and E. A. Shils (eds.), 'Towards a General Theory of Action' (New York, 1962) p. 180.

3. Cf. T. Parsons, 'Societies: Evolutionary and Comparative Perspectives' (Englewood Cliffs, 1968) p. 5.

4. Ibid., pp. 5–7. In earlier work on action systems, only three subsystems were distinguished and the organism was omitted: see, for example, Parsons and Shils, 'Towards a General Theory', esp. pp. 47–243.

5. It is in the most recent writings of Talcott Parsons that we find this homology thesis most fully elaborated. See, for example, T. Parsons, 'Systems Analysis: Social Systems', in 'International Encyclopedia of the Social Sciences', ed. R. Sills (New York, 1968) xv 458–72; 'Some Problems of General Theory', in 'Theoretical Sociology', ed. J. C. McKinney and E. A. Tiryakian (New York, 1970) pp. 26–68; and 'Societies', pp. 5–29.

6. Parsons, 'Societies', p. 28.

7. Cf. T. Parsons, 'An outline of the Social System', in 'Theories of Society', ed. T. Parsons, E. A. Shils, K. D. Naegele, J. R. Pitts (New York, 1961), pp. 30–79, esp. p. 73.

8. Ibid., pp. 71–2 and 74–7. Parsons distinguishes between process (involving no structural change), structural differentiation, radical dissolution of the social system and radical social change. Smelser also discusses four types of change: short-term decline, short-term reconstruction, long-term decline and long-term reconstruction or progress through differentiation ('Essays', pp. 192–280).

9. Cf. Smelser, 'Collective Behaviour', pp. 380–1; 'Essays', p. 266; and Parsons, in 'Theories of Society', pp. 70–1. This theoretical indeterminacy is due in part to the open rather than closed nature of the various systems involved and in part to the complexity of social change itself.

10. It is within this context that the more specific analysis of inflationary and deflationary processes in the interchange between differentiated functional subsystems must be considered: we discuss both types of process below.

11. Social strain is nowhere precisely defined by the normative functionalists. Two representative definitions are the following: 'an impairment of the relations among and consequently inadequate functioning of the components of action' (Smelser, 'Collective Behaviour', p. 47); and 'a condition in the *relation* between two or more structured units (i.e., subsystems of the system) that constitutes tendency or pressure toward changing that relation to one incompatible with the equilibrium of the relevant part of the system' (Parsons, 'Theories of Society', p. 71).

12. Marvin Scott has developed a theory of the social sources of alienation from this typology. Value strain produces extreme social isolation; normative strain produces underconformity, non-involved intimacy, anomie and mistrust; mobilisation strain leads to alienation from the role and to relative deprivation; and facilities strain produces a sense of powerlessness. Scott stresses also the indeterminacy between structured strain and alienation. Ackerman and Parsons have distinguished between alienation and anomie in somewhat similar terms: alienation is focused on commitment to role occupancy while anomie concerns the adequacy of normative specification of role requirements. See M. B. Scott, 'The Social Sources of Alienation', in 'The New Sociology', ed. I. L. Horowitz (New York, 1964), pp. 239–52; and C. Ackerman and T. Parsons, 'The Concept of "Social System" as a Theoretical Device', in 'Concepts, Theory and Explanation in the Behavioural Sciences', ed. G. J. DiRenzo (New York, 1966) pp. 24–40, esp. 34–40.

13. Smelser, 'Social Change', pp. 38–9. Smelser relates these three types of

disturbance to the creation of hysterical, wish-fulfilment, and hostile generalised beliefs respectively: see 'Collective Behaviour', pp. 84–109.

14. Smelser, 'Collective Behaviour', p. 71 (italics in original).
15. Ibid., pp. 8–9; Parsons and Smelser 'Economy and Society', pp. 236–7.
16. Ibid., pp. 80–130.
17. Ibid., pp. 83–4 and passim.
18. Smelser, 'Collective Behaviour, p. 69.
19. This sixth condition clearly implies that collective behaviour is also uninstitutionalised in the sense of derogated or proscribed by the centre: Smelser devotes little attention to this aspect of such behaviour.
20. For a discussion of the logic of value-added, see Smelser, 'Collective Behaviour', pp. 13–21, and 'Essays', pp. 210–11.
21. Cf. the definition of social movement proposed by Joseph Gusfield – 'socially shared activities and beliefs directed toward the demand for change in some aspect of the social order'. See J. R. Gusfield (ed.), 'Protest, Reform, and Revolt' (New York, 1970) p. 2; the definition is italicised in the original.
22. Smelser argues that such limitations are particularly common '(1) among politically disinherited peoples, especially recent migrants; (2) among colonially dominated peoples; (3) among persecuted minorities; (4) in inflexible political structures; (5) in post-revolutionary situations; (6) in situations marked by the failure of government by political parties' ('Collective Behaviour', p. 325).
23. Smelser, 'Essays', p. 273.
24. Ibid., pp. 273–6.
25. Ibid., p. 278.
26. On structural differentiation processes, see Parsons, in 'Theories of Society', pp. 70–9; 'Some Considerations on the Theory of Social Change', in 'Rural Sociology', xxvi (1961) 219–39; and 'Societies', pp. 21–5; and Smelser 'Social Change', passim, and 'Essays', pp. 243–54, 270, and 274–5.
27. Parsons, 'Sociological Theory and Modern Society', pp. 290–5, 341–5, 382. Smelser relates structural differentiation, media of exchange with more than a certain degree of liquidity, and rationality in the disposition of these media to the structural possibilities of craze collective behaviour ('Collective Behaviour', pp. 175–88).
28. Parsons, 'Sociological Theory and Modern Society', p. 276.
29. Ibid., p. 308.
30. Ibid., p. 283.
31. Ibid., p. 364; cf. T. Parsons, 'On the Concept of Value Commitments', 'Sociological Inquiry', xxxviii (1968) 135–60.
32. Parsons, 'Sociological Theory and Modern Society', pp. 269–70, 309–12, and 361–6.
33. Cf. Parsons, 'Sociological Theory and Modern Society', pp. 286–93 and 337–45. Parsons' analysis of power inflation is somewhat vague and the illustration of power deflation is actually drawn from the integrative system. An analysis similar in many ways to Parsons' discussion, but more intelligible, is to be found in K. W. Deutsch, 'The Nerves of Government' (New York, 1963) pp. 120–4. A less abstract analysis – which does not refer to coercion – is found in H. C. Bredemeier and R. M. Stephenson, 'The Analysis of Social Systems' (New York, 1962) pp. 387–91.
34. Parsons, 'Sociological Theory and Modern Society', pp. 381–2.
35. Cf. Parsons, in 'Sociological Inquiry', xxxviii (1968) 153–9.
36. For an examination of these other aspects, see M. Black (ed.), 'The Social Theories of Talcott Parsons' (Englewood Cliffs, 1961) and

Mitchell, 'Sociological Analysis and Politics'. The latter work reviews a number of Parsons' empirical applications as well as his theoretical framework.

37. Cf. R. Dahrendorf, 'Class and Class Conflict in Industrial Society' (London, 1959) and 'Conflict after Class' (London, 1967).

38. Cf. A. Gramsci, 'The Prince and other Essays' (New York, 1969). The 'New Left' also tends to this view: see, for example, P. Anderson and R. Blackburn (eds.), 'Towards Socialism' (London, 1965).

39. Dahrendorf employs Weber's definition of authority in developing his theory: this involves reference to the legitimacy of the specific commands of authority ('Class and Class Conflict', p. 237).

40. Cf. Parsons, 'Social System', pp. 39 and 141.

41. Cf. Gramsci, 'Modern Prince', pp. 169–75; and V. I. Lenin, 'What Is To Be Done?' (London, 1970 ed.) pp. 80–3, 102–11, 122–39, 149, and passim. Cf. 'Towards Socialism', pp. 223–47.

42. Cf. C. W. Mills, 'The Sociological Imagination' (Harmondsworth, 1970) pp. 45–56.

43. This is also true for more recent Marxist sociology: see, for example, the contributions to P. Berger (ed.), 'Marxism and Sociology' (New York, 1968) esp. at pp. 40, 65–6, and 80–1; and R. Miliband, 'The State and Capitalist Society' (London, 1969) p. 15.

44. The exact content of the superstructure is nowhere to be found in the literature. It makes most sense to treat it as a residual category of non-economic institutions and ideas – thus the law of contract is basic and family law is a superstructural phenomenon. As we move from the legal and political to the social, religious and ideological we move to areas increasingly superstructural in character.

45. Cf. K. Marx, 'A Contribution to the Critique of Political Economy' (Chicago, 1904) pp. 11–3; K. Marx and F. Engels, 'The German Ideology' (New York, 1967), pp. 6–12 and passim.

46. On joint-stock companies and co-operatives, see K. Marx, 'Capital', vol. iii (London, 1962) 431. The former resolve the antagonism between capitalists and proletariat negatively, the latter positively. For discussion, see S. Avinieri, 'Karl Marx: Social and Political Thought' (London, 1968) pp. 174–84; J. A. Banks, 'Marxist Sociology in Action' (London, 1970) pp. 30, 166, 95–7; and T. Nichols, 'Ownership, Control, and Ideology' (London, 1969).

47. Marx-Engels, 'German Ideology', p. 24; F. Engels, 'Origin of the Family, Private Property, and the State' (New York, 1942) pp. 154–8.

48. Marx-Engels, 'German Ideology', pp. 27–43.

49. See particularly F. Engels, Letter to Bloch, in K. Marx and F. Engels, 'Selected Correspondence' (Moscow, 1935) pp. 498–500.

50. Cf. K. Marx and F. Engels, 'Communist Manifesto' (London, 1948 ed.) pp. 119–35.

51. It is often noted that Marx's historical studies display a greater variety of classes and conflict groups than is implied in the basic dichotomy of capitalist and wage-earner; and also that the unfinished chapter on class in 'Capital' mentions three classes – capitalist, wage-labourer and landowner. These difficulties can be explained in terms of the trend towards polarisation, as yet incomplete, that Marx appears to have derived from his understanding of the dynamics of capitalism.

52. Marx-Engels, 'Communist Manifesto', pp. 126–7; Marx, 'Capital', vol. iii 244–59.

53. For a discussion of these three phenomena, see G. Lichtheim, 'Marxism' (London, 1964 ed.) and C. W. Mills, 'The Marxists' (Harmondsworth, 1963) pp. 86–90.

54. Marx-Engels, 'Communist Manifesto', pp. 129–33.
55. K. Marx and F. Engels, 'On Britain' (London, 1962) pp. 494–5.
56. Marx and Engels, 'Communist Manifesto', pp. 155–8; this manifesto presents an early and schematic outline of the course of the proletarian revolution in which all six stages can be identified.
57. We are concerned here with sociologically important revisions and not with the more general history of 'revisionism' in Marxist theory – on which see Lichtheim, 'Marxism', pp. 278–300.
58. Cf. Dahrendorf, 'Class and Class Conflict', esp. pp. 237–40; and 'Toward a Theory of Social Conflict', in 'Journal of Conflict Resolution', 2 (1958) 170–83.
59. Dahrendorf, 'Conflict After Class', p. 8.
60. Ibid., pp. 8–15.
61. Ibid., pp. 15–24.
62. See 'Class and Class Conflict', pp. 218–23.
63. Marx and Engels were not of course entirely neglectful of these factors. They note a similar phenomenon in the refugee serfs who sought individual advancement within the feudal formation at the expense of a general abolition of the serf class (cf. 'German Ideology', p. 78). Engels notes the importance of mobility and immigration in retarding the development of class consciousness in the United States: see Marx-Engels, 'On Britain', pp. 6–7n.
64. Cf. Stretton, 'The Political Sciences', p. 332.
65. Cf. M. Olson, jr., 'The Logic of Collective Action: Public Goods and the Theory of Groups' (Cambridge, Mass., 1965) passim.
66. Cf. V. I. Lenin, 'The State and Revolution', in 'The Essential Left' (London, 1960) p. 152.
67. Engels, 'Origin of the Family', pp. 157–8; Lenin, 'State and Revolution', mentions the Kerensky government as a third example of this phenomenon (p. 158).
68. Marx-Engels, 'On Britain', p. 353; cf. R. Miliband, 'Marx and The State', in 'Socialist Register, 1965', ed. R. Miliband and J. Saville (London, 1965) pp. 278–96 esp. 283–5.
69. Engels, 'Origin of the Family', pp. 154–5.
70. Cf. Miliband, in 'Socialist Register', p. 287; and G. Lichtheim, 'Marx and the Asiatic Mode of Production', in 'St Antony's Papers', xiv (1963) 86–112.
71. Cf. K. A. Wittfogel, 'Oriental Despotism' (New Haven, 1957) pp. 372–412, for an analysis of these developments.
72. Lenin, 'State and Revolution', passim.
73. Ibid., p. 181.
74. Lenin, 'What Is To Be Done?', passim.
75. In rejecting economism Gramsci draws on Lukacs' emphasis on the independent role of class consciousness: see G. Lukacs, 'History and Class Consciousness' (London, 1970).
76. Cf. Gramsci, 'Modern Prince', passim. For commentaries on Gramsci, much of whose work is not available in English translation, see: G. Williams, 'The Concept of "Egemonia" in the Thought of Gramsci', in 'Journal of the History of Ideas', xxi (1960) 586–99; J. Merrington, 'Theory and Practice in Gramsci's Marxism', in 'Socialist Register, 1968', ed. R. Miliband and J. Saville (London, 1968) 145–76; and, more generally, J. Cammett, 'Antonio Gramsci and the Origins of Italian Communism' (Stanford, 1967).
77. Cf. P. M. Blau, 'Exchange and Power in Social Life' (New York, 1964) pp. 2 and 12–4; G. C. Homans, 'Social Behaviour: its elementary

forms' (London, 1962) pp. 378–96; W. J. Goode, 'A Theory of Role Strain', in 'American Sociological Review', xxv (1960) 483–96.

78. It is for this reason that we examine mainly Blau's contributions to the theoretical study of exchange and neglect works that focus largely on the microsocial level: see, for example, Homans, 'Social Behaviour', and J. W. Thibaut and H. H. Kelley, 'The Social Psychology of Groups' (New York, 1959).

79. Blau, 'Exchange and Power', p. 5.

80. Ibid., pp. 312–13.

81. Ibid., p. 267.

82. Ibid., pp. 278–80.

83. Blau treats stratification as an institutional mechanism for structuring economic incentives and class as actual collectivities with differential wealth, power and prestige (pp. 278–9). But deference seems to be the macrosocial equivalent of esteem in the small group: cf. Homans, 'Social Behaviour', p. 379.

84. Blau, 'Exchange and Power', pp. 118–25.

85. Cf. Blau, 'Exchange and Power', pp. 208–13. See also Blau's 'Critical Remarks on Weber's Theory of Authority', in 'American Political Science Review', lvii (1963) 305–16.

86. Blau, 'Exchange and Power', pp. 227–52. Blau cites Dahrendorf in his discussion of opposition and there are many parallels (p. 250n.).

87. A. W. Gouldner, 'The Norm of Reciprocity', in 'American Sociological Review', xxv (1960) 161–78; Blau, 'Exchange and Power', pp. 92–3.

88. Cf. the discussion of Homans in W. G. Runciman, 'Justice, Congruence, and Professor Homans', in 'European Journal of Sociology', viii (1967) 115–28; and Homans, 'Social Behaviour', pp. 243–64.

89. Blau, 'Exchange and Power', pp. 279–80. Cf. S. N. Eisenstadt, 'Institutionalisation and Change', in 'American Sociological Review', xxix (1964) 49–59.

90. Blau, 'Exchange and Power', pp. 117–9; 313–4, and passim.

91. Wagner provides an important discussion of emergence and its significance for sociological theory construction in his article on the fallacy of displaced scope: see H. R. Wagner, 'The Displacement of Scope', in 'American Journal of Sociology', lxix (1963–4) 571–84.

92. Blau, 'Exchange and Power', pp. 253–73. Homans also stresses the role of social approval and esteem as generalised reinforcers of social organisation: see 'Social Behaviour', p. 380 and passim.

93. Blau, 'Exchange and Power', pp. 273–6; cf. Stinchcombe, 'Constructing Social Theory', pp. 181–8.

94. Cf. R. L. Curry and L. L. Wade, 'A Theory of Political Exchange' (Englewood Cliffs, 1968) pp. 51–71. Elsewhere the authors develop political models of perfect competition, oligopoly and monopoly.

95. Cf. W. C. Mitchell, 'The Shape of Political Theory to Come: from Political Sociology to Political Economy', in 'American Behavioral Scientist', xi (1967) 8–37.

96. For an examination of several such models, see B. M. Barry, 'Sociologists, Economists, and Democracy' (London, 1969) passim; for a useful discussion of market and plan rationality, see Dahrendorf, 'Essays', pp. 215–31.

97. Cf. Olson, 'The Logic of Collective Action', pp. 102–10 and passim.

3   Some Emergent Themes in the Study of Order

1. Illustrative of the first approach is D. Lockwood, 'Social Integration and System Integration', in 'Explorations in Social Change', ed. G. K.

Zollschan and W. Hirsch (London, 1964), pp. 244–56; and P. van den Berghe, 'Dialectic and Functionalism', in 'American Sociological Review', xxviii (1963) 695–705. The second type of conclusion is found in Dahrendorf, 'Class and Class Conflict', p. 163; J. A. Rex, 'Key Problems in Sociological Theory' (London, 1961) p. 112; Parsons, 'Structure and Process', p. 173; and Blau, 'Exchange and Power', p. 13. The third conclusion is nowhere fully developed but it is more or less implicit in A. Giddens, 'Power in the Recent Writings of Talcott Parsons', in 'Sociology', ii (1968) 256–72; I. L. Horowitz, 'Consensus, Conflict, and Cooperation', in 'Social Forces', xli (1962) 177–88; and P. Cohen, 'Modern Social Theory (London, 1968), pp. 166–72.

2. G. Lenski, 'Power and Privilege' (New York, 1966) constitutes one attempt at synthesis on the level of stratification systems; L. Coser, 'The Functions of Social Conflict' (New York, 1956) applies functionalism to the area of social conflict.

3. Indeed W. L. Wallace classifies the three theories as functional structuralism, conflict structuralism and exchange structuralism: see his 'Sociological Theory' (London, 1969) pp. 25–34.

4. For a useful discussion of the 'residual category' and the importance of its elimination in scientific progress, see T. Parsons, 'Structure of Social Action', especially pp. 16–9.

5. Both Parsons and Lockwood stress the codetermination of actual behaviour by norms and realistic exigencies, by norms and factual substratum: see Parsons, 'Structure and Process', p. 172; and D. Lockwood, 'Some Remarks on "The Social System"', in 'British Journal of Sociology', vii (1956) 134–46. Cf. also N. Gross et al., 'Explorations in Role Analysis' (New York, 1958) pp. 281–319.

6. See T. Parsons and W. White, 'The Link Between Character and Society', in 'Culture and Social Character', ed. S. M. Lipset and L. Lowenthal (New York, 1961) especially pp. 101–2; Parsons, 'A Revised Analytical Approach to Social Stratification', in 'Essays in Sociological Theory', especially pp. 393 and 415–6; Parsons, 'Social Strains in America', in 'Structure and Process', especially pp. 232–4 and 246–7; Parsons, in 'Sociological Inquiry', xxxviii (1968) 156–9; and Parsons, in 'Theories of Society', pp. 70–9.

7. Parsons, 'Societies', p. 22.

8. Engels argues that law, for example, displays a strain to consistency that leads it away from strict class-oriented justice: see Engels' letter to Conrad Schmidt, in Marx-Engels, 'Selected Correspondence', pp. 480–3. More generally, see M. Kalab, 'The Specificity of the Marxist Conception of Sociology', in 'Marxism and Sociology', pp. 58–76, especially 68–9.

9. For a discussion of double contingency in love relations, see Blau, 'Exchange and Power', pp. 76–85; and, more generally, Parsons, 'Social System', pp. 30 and 36–7.

10. Except, possibly, in communist society.

11. Parsons, 'Sociological Theory and Modern Society', pp. 277–8.

12. Blau, 'Exchange and Power', p. 30.

13. For a theoretical model within the normative functionalist framework which treats the solidarity of social systems as variable and examine its consequences, see O. Ramsoy, 'Social Groups as System and Subsystem' (New York, 1963) passim. For a similar exercise within the constraint framework, see J. A. Von Doorn, 'Conflict in Formal Organisations', in 'Conflict and Society', ed. J. de Rueck and H. Knight (London, 1964) pp. 107–32.

14. Marx, 'Capital', vol. iii 380.

15. It is possible to convert the functional problems into a sanctions-oriented set: thus a social system to be orderly and stable must regulate the use of all four sanctions. The alternative is arbitrary intervention and exploitation. Some societies obviously manage these problems better than others.

16. The theory of surplus value and the assumptions underlying it constitute the most problematic aspect of classical Marxist theory from the viewpoint of the would-be synthesist. For parallels in other functional systems, see Jessop, in 'Sociological Review', xvii (1969) 421.

17. See, for example, Engels' letter to Schmidt, in Marx and Engels, 'Selected Correspondence', pp. 480–3.

18. Marx, 'Capital', vol. i, part iv passim.

19. K. Marx and F. Engels, 'The Holy Family' (Moscow, 1956) p. 149.

20. See, for example, E. J. Hobsbawm, 'Primitive Rebels' (Manchester, 1959) and P. M. Worsley, 'The Trumpet Shall Sound', 2nd ed. (London, 1968), for two Marxian analyses of such phenomena.

21. Particularly as the first two involve a different level of system reference – to the social movement rather than the more inclusive societal system.

22. See Chapter 1 above for a brief outline of these terms.

23. Parsons, 'Societies', p. 23.

24. Cf. Parsons, in 'International Encyclopedia of Social Sciences', pp. 464, 470.

25. Cf. H. Marcuse, 'One-Dimensional Man' (London, 1968) and 'Repressive Tolerance', in 'A Critique of Pure Tolerance', written with R. P. Wolff and B. Moore (London, 1969).

26. K. Marx, 'On the Jewish Question', in 'Early Writings', ed. T. B. Bottomore (London, 1963).

27. Ibid., p. 29.

28. Cf. Marx-Engels, 'German Ideology', p. 77.

29. Cf. Parsons, 'Sociological Theory and Modern Society', pp. 113–5; he refers to these two difficulties as the Durkheim and Weber problems respectively. Cf. 'Societies', p. 112 n.

30. Parsons, 'Sociological Theory and Modern Society', pp. 115–6.

31. See, for example, Mills, 'The Marxists', pp. 104–5.

32. Cf. P. Anderson, 'Origins of the Present Crisis', in 'Towards Socialism', pp. 11–52, esp. p. 42. Anderson argues that in the long term power coincides with control of the means of production; in the short term power can be predominantly military, bureaucratic, economic, ideological or even legislative.

33. Cf. B. M. Barry, 'Political Argument' (London, 1965) pp. 173–86; and Cohen, 'Modern Social Theory', pp. 115–8.

34. Constant-sum situations refer to situations in which the utilities from various outcomes for different actors always total to a constant amount. Zero-sum is a special case: it refers to a situation in which one actor gains utility in exact correspondence to another's disutility.

35. Lockwood suggests one way of generalising the substratum concept in his discussion of normative functionalism. He distinguishes between the material substratum (the factual disposition of means) and the normative order (the normative definition of the situation) and argues that these can be more or less antagonistic. We propose that each functional sub-system could be analysed in terms of the factual disposition of sanctions and the normative order and in terms of the relative antagonism between them for different classes of actor. See Lockwood, in 'British Journal of Sociology', vii (1956) 136.

4   A Conceptual Framework

1. Cf. S. F. Nadel, 'The Theory of Social Structure' (London, 1957) pp. 114–24; and E. A. Nordlinger, 'The Working Class Tories' (London, 1967) p. 14.

2. See, for example, E. A. Shils, 'Centre and Periphery', in 'The Logic of Personal Knowledge', ed. M. Polanyi (London, 1961) pp. 117–30; S. N. Eisenstadt, 'Prestige, Participation, and Strata-Formation', in 'Social Stratification', ed. J. A. Jackson (London, 1968) pp. 62–103; D. Lerner, 'Some Comments on Centre-Periphery Relations', in 'Comparing Nations', ed. R. L. Merritt and S. Rokkan (New Haven, 1968) pp. 259–65; S. M. Lipset and S. Rokkan (eds.), 'Party Systems and Voter Alignments' (New York, 1967) pp. 33–49; Stinchcombe, 'Constructing Social Theories', pp. 173–80; Curry and Wade, 'Political Exchange', pp. 22–3; J. P. Nettl and R. Robertson, 'International Systems and the Modernisation of Societies' (London, 1967) passim; T. Parsons and G. M. Platt, 'Considerations on the American Academic System', in 'Minerva', vi (1968) 497–523 and pp. 512–3.

3. See especially Shils, in 'Logic of Personal Knowledge', p. 117.

4. Cf. F. Parkin, 'Middle Class Radicalism' (Manchester, 1968) pp. 21–5, for an illustration of this circularity.

5. Cf. the suggested operationalisation of Nadel's analysis of social structure in M. Freilich, 'Toward a Model of Social Structure', in 'Journal of the Royal Anthropological Institute', xciv (1964) 183–200.

6. Cf. J. M. Yinger, 'Subculture and Contraculture', in 'American Sociological Review', xxv (1960) 625–35; and C. A. Valentine, 'Culture and Poverty' (Chicago, 1968) pp. 104–13.

7. This is in contradistinction to Parsons' particularistic usage in which power is only one of four types of constraint.

8. Cf. R. A. Dahl, 'The Concept of Power', in 'Behavioral Science', ii (1957) 201–15. More generally, see R. Bell, D. V. Edwards and R. Wagner (eds.), 'Political Power' (New York, 1969).

9. These preference structures will of course reflect the individual's commitments, and commitments are one type of sanction; it follows that complete control over commitments is the most effective basis of power and that other types are effective only to the extent that cultural control is incomplete.

10. 'Basic force', 'force activation', 'force depletion' and 'force conditioning' models of power relations are discussed in J. G. March, 'The Power of Power', in 'Varieties of Political Theory', ed. D. Easton (Englewood Cliffs, 1966), pp. 39–70.

11. It is in fact these situations that Parsons incorrectly identifies as a breakthrough from the zero-sum constraint.

12. Dahl, in 'Behavioral Science', ii (1957) 201–15.

13. 'Authorisation' is preferable to 'power' because of our generic usage of the latter term and because it points more clearly to the symbolic nature and political character of the medium (cf. the term 'influence' for symbolic social power).

14. A similar point is made by T. S. Turner in his paper on the symbolic media: see 'Parsons' Concept of "Generalised Media of Social Interaction" and its Relevance for Social Anthropology', in 'Sociological Inquiry', xxxviii (1968) 121–34.

15. On pecuniary systems of status attribution, see D. Lockwood, 'Sources of Variation in Working-Class Images of Society', in 'Sociological Review', xiv (1966) 249–67.

16. Many writers talk of the 'power of organisation' and Lockwood includes control over the means of organisation in his general definition of sub-stratum; it should be clear that organisation has a dual reference – to both the division of labour in any power base and to the pattern of control over the power base. The context or a more precise phrase should make our reference clear below.

17. Cf. R. H. Turner. 'Sponsored and Contest Mobility in the School System', in 'American Sociological Review', xxv (1960) 855–67.

18. Cf. R. Williams, 'Communications' Harmondsworth, 1968 ed.) pp 116–24.

19. Cf. S. Andreski, 'Military Organisation and Society' (London, 1968 ed.) passim.

20. The resistance to such innovations in the development of English secondary education, including most recently opposition to comprehensivisation, can be interpreted at least in part in these terms: see, for example, O. Banks, 'The Sociology of Education' (London, 1968) pp. 22–8.

21. For a penetrating discussion of economic rationality and its relation to actual institutional economies, see K. Polanyi et al., 'Trade and Market in the Early Empires' (New York, 1957) pp. 239–319.

22. 'Secondary' and 'tertiary' here refer to the power base and not to the type of economic activity – manufacturing or service industries – as is more usually the case.

23. For a discussion of the complexities of economic class relations in advanced industrial societies, see J. Pen, 'Harmony and Conflict in Modern Society' (London, 1966) passim.

24. This situation exactly parallels that for peasant societies in conflict over property in land. It is mistaken to argue that economic conflict is zero-sum only in the latter case, variable-sum in industrial societies owing to variation in productivity: for such an argument, see Huntington, 'Political Order', pp. 298–9.

25. For a discussion of these conflicts and their impact on peasant society, see G. M. Foster, 'Peasant Society and the Image of Limited Good', in 'American Anthropologist', lxii (1965) 293–315.

26. If the 'authorities' are able to employ non-political means to support their commands, then they cease to that extent to be authorities and belong to other power centres.

27. Andreski, 'Military Organisation', provides an important discussion of the relations between these factors.

28. This relationship parallels that between capitalists and managers in the economy and poses similar problems concerning the possibility of a managerial revolution.

29. Cf. Janowitz, 'Military in Political Development', passim; S. P. Huntington (ed.), 'Changing Patterns of Military Politics' (New York, 1962); and J. A. Van Doorn (ed.), 'Military and Society' (The Hague, 1970).

30. The distribution of protection, and where authority is institutionalised, of policy benefits, defines the political equivalent of 'income classes' and thus structures conflicts of interest.

31. Cf. S. N. Eisenstadt, 'Primitive Political Systems', in 'American Anthropologist', lxi (1959) 200–20; and D. Easton, 'Political Anthropology', in 'Biennial Review of Anthropology', ed. H. Siegel (New York, 1959) pp. 210–62.

32. Non-political organisations are also frequently designated 'bureaucratic' on account of their organisational character but they are based on political authority only in so far as non-compliance can be sanctioned

directly or indirectly through coercion. The use of contract is an important means of obtaining such support indirectly through the interest of the State in enforcing contract law. Other sanctions, however, are generally more important. See Parsons and Smelser, 'Economy and Society'; Etzioni, 'Comparative Analysis of Complex Organisations', pp. 23–67.

33. Cf. Dahrendorf, 'Class and Class Conflict', passim.
34. Cf. S. N. Eisenstadt, 'Introduction', in M. Weber, 'Charisma and Institution Building' (Chicago, 1968) pp. xxxiii–iv.
35. Cf. Eisenstadt, in 'Social Stratification', pp. 69–76.
36. Cf. M. G. Smith, 'Pre-Industrial Stratification Systems', in 'Social Structure and Mobility in Economic Development', ed. N. J. Smelser and S. M. Lipset (London, 1966) pp. 141–76; and Lenski, 'Power and Privilege', pp. 102–12.
37. Such attempts can be observed in all social strata ranging from the monopolistic tendencies of skilled unions and the professions to the ritual or legal exclusivity of castes and estates.
38. See, for example, J. A. Galtung, 'A Structural Theory of Aggression', in 'Journal of Peace Research', i (1965) 95–119; I. W. Goffman, 'Status Inconsistency and Preference for Change in Power', in 'American Sociological Review', xxii (1957) 275–81; D. Bell (ed.), 'The Radical Right' (New York, 1964). For a critique, see S. Box and J. Ford, 'Some Questionable Assumptions in the Theory of Status Inconsistency', in 'Sociological Review', xvii (1969) 191–8.
39. The reader versed in Parsonian theory will have noticed that we have ignored the 'latency inputs' into the political and social systems, as well as such inputs other than land in the economy, in our discussion of different classes in these systems. These inputs are in fact defined as commitments to activity independent of short-term rewards and are thus controlled by the cultural system. Parsons ignores this definition and treats labour as well as land as inputs from the latency system. See Parsons and Smelser, 'Economy and Society', pp. 25, 70, 114–23, and 125n.
40. It should be emphasised that these are only approximations: civilian authorities are rarely peripheral in other than a military sense and even 'democratic' systems rarely display commitment to the interests of all members of a society.
41. Cf. Marx and Engels, 'German Ideology', p. 20 and passim.
42. Where such technology is absent or is controlled by non-political centres, then physical repression and conflict with the cultural centre are likely political results: see S. N. Eisenstadt, 'Religious Organisations and Political Process in Centralised Empires', in 'Journal of Asian Studies', xxi (1962) 271–94.
43. The process underlying such increasing hierarchisation may be called 'objectification': it occurs where the output of a system becomes a further means of control over the periphery, e.g., when a worker's productivity adds to the stock of capital, or commitments increase the legitimacy of the cultural system. See my paper, 'Exchange and Power in Structural Analysis', in 'Sociological Review', xxvii (1969) 415–37.
44. Cf. Homans, 'Social Behaviour', pp. 60, 71–2, and passim.
45. For attempts at developing such measures for the economy, see P. Sraffa, 'The Production of Commodities by Commodities' (Cambridge, 1963) and J. Robinson, 'Pierro Sraffa and the Rate of Exploitation', in 'New Left Review', xxxi (1965) 28–34.
46. Such an approach is implied by Robinson, in 'New Left Review', xxxi (1965).

47. See Chapters 5, 6 and 7 for a discussion of these factors.
48. Cf. Parsons' notion of moral responsibility, in 'Sociological Enquiry', xxxviii (1968) 137–8; and F. G. Bailey, 'Stratagems and Spoils' (Oxford, 1969) pp. 37 and 43.
49. Where social and cultural centres are strong, lack of compliance is likely to be sanctioned by peripheral admonitions as well as central derogation.
50. This assumes that there has been no surplus from the previous period with which to reward the periphery.
51. This assumes an absolute objective standard for measuring exploitation: subjective or relative objective methods imply different definitions of exploitation (see above).
52. Cf. M. Sahlins, 'On the Sociology of Primitive Exchange', in 'The Relevance of Models to Social Anthropology', ed. M. Banton (London, 1965) pp. 139–236; N. J. Smelser, 'A Comparative View of Exchange Systems', in 'Economic Development and Cultural Change', vii (1959) 173–82; and Polanyi et al., 'Trade and Market', passim.
53. Feudal serfdom, slavery, early monasticism, tithing, are four examples of this phenomenon.
54. S. Andreski, 'Parasitism and Subversion' (London, 1966).
55. Cf. R. D. Jessop, 'Civility and Traditionalism in English Political Culture', in 'British Journal of Political Science', i (1971) 1–24.
56. Cf. R. A. Dahl (ed.), 'Political Oppositions in Western Democracies' (New Haven, 1966), pp. 371–86.
57. Cf. T. Parsons, 'Pattern Variables Revisited', in 'American Sociological Review', xxv (1960) 467–83.
58. For discussion of secularisation and its concomitants, see: D. Apter, 'The Role of Traditionalism in the Political Modernisation of Ghana and Uganda', in 'World Politics', xiii (1959) 45–68; G. Almond and B. Powell, 'Comparative Politics' (Boston, 1966) pp. 60–4; H. Becker, 'Sacred and Secular Societies', in 'Through Values to Social Interpretation', ed. H. Becker (Duke, 1950) pp. 248–80; Bellah, in 'American Sociological Review', xxiv (1958); Eisenstadt, in 'Charisma and Institution-Building', lv; and Parsons, in 'Sociological Enquiry', xxxviii (1968) 150–9.
59. Cf. Nettl and Robertson, 'International Systems and Modernisation', p. 46.
60. For those who like spatial analogies, it is suggested that institutional integration is the major horizontal dimension of culture systems, consensus the major vertical dimension.
61. Cf. Stinchcombe, 'Constructing Social Theories', pp. 181–8.
62. Gurr, 'Why Men Rebel', pp. 274–317, provides evidence on this.
63. For a detailed discussion, see D. Katz and E. Stotland, 'A Preliminary Statement to a Theory of Attitude Change', in 'Psychology', ed. S. Koch (New York, 1959), vol. iii 243–76.
64. The evidence is assembled in Mann, in 'American Sociological Review', xxxv (1970) passim.

5 A Theory of Order, Reform and Revolution

1. It is the actors' perception of legitimacy that is important here and not the legitimacy of the expectations in terms of the dominant value system.
2. The radical escalation of dissent in such circumstances is too well known to require documentation; on the 'return to normalcy', see Brinton, 'Anatomy', pp. 215–50; Leiden and Schmidt, 'Politics of

Violence', pp. 66–7; and L. P. Edwards, 'The Natural History of Revolution' (Chicago, 1927) pp. 186–209.

3. Gurr has reviewed the evidence for these assumptions in depth in his book, 'Why Men Rebel', pp. 59–91.
4. Deprivation must therefore be distinguished from exploitation – deprivation is a subjective phenomenon while exploitation is an objectively defined measure of exchange rates. The two phenomena are analytically distinct even though they tend to covary.
5. For further discussion and for illustrations of contradictions in social structure, see: L. Althusser, 'Contradiction and Overdetermination', in 'New Left Review', 41 (1967) 15–35; M. Godelier, 'System, Structure, and Contradiction in "Capital"', in 'Socialist Register 1967', ed. R. Miliband and J. Saville (London, 1967) pp. 91–119; and S. N. Eisenstadt, 'Internal Contradictions in Bureaucratic Polities', in 'Comparative studies in Society and History', i (1958) 58–75.
6. Cf. Gurr, 'Why Men Rebel', pp. 46–58, for an analysis of different types of deprivation: decremental (constant expectations, falling gratifications), aspirational (rising expectations, constant gratifications), and progressive (rising expectations, falling gratifications).
7. Cf. L. Trotsky, 'The Russian Revolution' (New York, 1959) p. 90.
8. Cf. Lenin, 'What Is To Be Done?', passim; and Gramsci, 'The Modern Prince', pp. 168–73.
9. For a discussion of the importance of 'dual power' in revolutionary situations, see Trotsky, 'Russian Revolution', pp. 199–208.
10. This is forcefully argued by Regis Debray in 'Revolution in the Revolution?' (Harmondsworth, 1968) passim.
11. Cf. F. Machlup, 'Another View of Cost-Push and Demand-Pull Inflation', in 'Review of Economics and Statistics', lxii (1960) 125–39; and the discussion in Chapter 2 above.
12. Cf. C. S. Belshaw, 'Traditional Exchange and Modern Markets' (Englewood Cliffs, 1965) pp. 20–9.

6 Studies in Order, Reform and Revolution – I

1. On this and other aspects of the band, see: V. G. Childe, 'What Happened in History' (Harmondsworth, 1964 ed.) pp. 33–54; Lenski, 'Power and Privilege', pp. 94–116; Sahlins, in 'Themes in Economic Anthropology'; I. Schapera, 'Government and Politics in Tribal Societies' (London, 1956) passim; E. R. Service, 'The Hunters' (Englewood Cliffs, 1966); Turner, in 'Sociological Enquiry', xxxviii (1968); Parsons, 'Societies', pp. 30–41. Not all band societies are based on kin groups but their dynamics are the same: see Walter, 'Terror and Resistance', pp. 62–3.
2. On lineage systems see: M. Fortes, 'The Structure of Unilineal Descent Groups', in 'American Anthropologist', lv (1953) 17–41; M. G. Smith, 'On Segmentary Lineage Systems', in 'Journal of the Royal Anthropological Institute', lxxxvi, 2 (1956) 39–80; and J. Middleton and D. Tait (eds.) 'Tribes Without Rulers' (London, 1958) pp. 1–31.
3. See, for example: E. E. Evans-Pritchard, 'The Nuer' (Oxford, 1940); M. Fortes, 'The Dynamics of Clanship among the Tallensi' (London, 1945); M. Gluckman, 'Custom and Conflict in Africa' (London, 1956) esp. pp. 1–28; J. Middleton, 'Lugbara Religion' (London, 1960); Middleton and Tait, 'Tribes Without Rulers'; K. F. and S. C. Otterbein, 'An Eye for an Eye, a Tooth for a Tooth', in 'American Anthropologist', lxvii (1965) 1470–82; and K. F. Otterbein, 'Internal

Wars: a cross-cultural study', in 'American Anthropologist', lxx (1968) 277–89.

4. See, for example, Eisenstadt, in 'American Anthropologist', lxi (1959) 205–10; and L. Krader, 'The Emergence of the State' (Englewood Cliffs, 1968), pp. 29–42.

5. See the important study by E. R. Leach, 'Political Systems of Highland Burma' (London, 1964 ed.) passim.

6. Cf. J. Goody, 'Technology, Tradition, and the State in Africa' (London, 1971), for a discussion of the important differences between African states and medieval European feudalism in terms of both economic and military technology.

7. Cf. E. Evans-Pritchard and M. Fortes (eds.), 'African Political Systems' (London, 1940) esp. pp. 11–4; Krader, 'Emergence of State', pp. 29–41; Walter, 'Terror and Resistance', pp. 56–108; L. Mair, 'Primitive Government' (Harmondsworth, 1962) passim; J. Beattie, 'Checks on the Abuse of Political Power in Some African States', in 'Sociologus', ix (1959) 97–115.

8. Cf. M. Gluckman, 'Politics, Law, and Ritual in Tribal Society' (Oxford, 1965) pp. 123–43; Schapera, 'Politics and Government', passim; L. A. Fallers, 'Despotism, Status Culture, and Social Mobility in an African Kingdom', in 'Comparative Studies in Society and History', ii (1959) 11–32; and L. Mair, 'Primitive Government', passim.

9. Cf. Lenski, 'Power and Privilege', pp. 164–8.

10. See particularly Gluckman, 'Politics, Law, and Ritual', pp. 144–63, where these different processes are discussed and illustrated; also, S. F. Nadel, 'A Black Byzantium' (London, 1940) pp. 69–146.

11. The segmentary state is intermediate between the classical segmentary lineage society and the fully centralised unitary state; its range is considerable – from the Shilluk to feudal and imperial systems. See A. W. Southall, 'Alur Society' (Cambridge, 1956) pp. 243–63 and passim.

12. Cf. Walter, 'Terror and Resistance', pp. 99 and 102–8; Krader, 'Formation of the State', pp. 38–42.

13. Cf. Lenski, 'Power and Privilege', pp. 165–6.

14. Cf. Walter, 'Terror and Resistance', esp. pp. 133–77 and 244–63; the hegemony was incomplete, however, and following Shaka's assassination the system became less despotic.

15. Cf. Eisenstadt, in 'Comparative Studies in Society and History', i (1958) 58–75; and the same author's book, 'The Political Systems of Empires' (New York, 1963) passim.

16. Cf. B. Moore, Jr., 'Social Origins of Dictatorship and Democracy' (London, 1967) pp. 330–41, 378–85, and 469–70.

17. Cf. E. R. Leach (ed.), 'Aspects of Caste in South India, Ceylon, and North-West Pakistan' (London, 1960); F. G. Bailey, 'Caste and the Economic Frontier' (Manchester, 1957) and 'Closed Social Stratification in India', in 'European Journal of Sociology', iv (1963) 107–25; M. N. Srinivas, 'A Note on Sanskritisation and Westernisation', in 'Far Eastern Quarterly', xv (1955), 492–96; P. M. Kolenda, 'Toward a Model of the Hindu "Jajmani" System', in 'Human Organisation', xxii (1963) 11–31; A. de Rueck and J. Knight (eds.), 'Caste and Race' (London, 1967); and L. Dumont, 'Homo Hierarchicus' (London, 1970).

18. Cf. Marx, 'Capital', i 357–8; Leach, in 'Aspects of Caste', pp. 6–10; Moore, 'Social Origins', pp. 330–41 and 469–70; but see also Bailey, in 'European Journal of Sociology', iv (1963), 107–41, and Konda, in 'Human Organisation', xxii (1963) passim.

19. Cf. Moore, 'Social Origins', pp. 341–70; A. R. Desai, 'The Social

Background to Indian Nationalism' (Bombay, 1948); and T. R. Metcalf, 'The Aftermath of Revolt: India 1857–1870' (Princeton, 1965) passim.

20. Cf. U. Patnaik, 'Peasant Mobilisation in India and China' (mimeo, 1969) p. 9; and Moore, 'Social Origins', pp. 378–85.

21. This process is clearly parallel to (although more complex than) that of genealogical redefinition and lineage realignments in segmentary lineage societies; both processes are due to emergent contradictions of one kind or another.

22. Cf. L. I. and S. H. Rudolf, 'The Political Role of India's Caste Associations', in 'Pacific Affairs', xxxiii (1960) 5–22; and also Bailey, in 'European Journal of Sociology', iv (1963) 107–41.

23. Cf. Moore, 'Social Origins', pp. 330–41 and 452–83; and also G. D. Berreman, 'Caste in India and the United States', in 'American Journal of Sociology', lxvi (1960) 120–7.

7 Studies in Order, Reform and Revolution – II

1. See particularly Eisenstadt, 'Political Systems', and Moore, 'Social Origins'; these two studies are complementary – the former deals with the general characteristics of the empires, the latter with the specifics of a smaller number.

2. For further discussion, see Eisenstadt, in 'Comparative Studies in Society and History', i (1958) 58–75.

3. On the background and course of the Chinese Communist revolution, see: H. Alavi, 'Peasants and Revolution', in 'Socialist Register 1965', ed. R. Miliband and J. Saville (London, 1965) pp. 241–77; M. Bernal, 'China' (unpubd 1969); J. Ch'en, 'Mao and the Chinese Revolution' (London, 1965); J. K. Fairbank, 'The United States and China' (Cambridge, Mass., 1959); C. P. Fitzgerald, 'The Birth of Communist China' (Harmondsworth, 1964); J. P. Harrison, 'The Communists and Chinese Peasant Rebellions' (London, 1969); R. Hofheinz, 'The Ecology of Chinese Communist Success', in 'Chinese Communist Politics in Action', ed. A. D. Barnett (Seattle, 1969) pp. 3–77; C. J. Johnson, 'Peasant Nationalism and Communist Power' (Stanford, 1962); Moore, 'Social Origins', pp. 162–227; F. Schurman and O. Schell (eds.), 'China Readings' (Harmondsworth, 1968); E. Snow, 'Red Star Over China' (London, 1938); and R. H. Tawney, 'Land and Labour in China' (London, 1932).

4. For the background and course of the conflicts in Northern Ireland, see particularly: D. P. Barritt and C. F. Carter, 'The Northern Ireland Problem' (London, 1962); Devlin, 'Price of My Soul'; O. D. Edwards, 'The Sins of Our Fathers' (Dublin, 1970); L. de Paor, 'Divided Ulster' (Harmondsworth, 1970); P. Gibbon, 'The Dialectic of Religion and Class in Ulster', in 'New Left Review', 55 (1970) 20–41; I. Hamilton, 'Irish Tangle', in 'Conflict Studies', 6 (1970); O'Neill, 'Ulster at the Cross-Roads'; and two reports of commissions appointed by the Governor of Northern Ireland – 'Disturbances in Northern Ireland' (Belfast, 1969) and 'Police in Northern Ireland' (Belfast, 1969).

5. Huntington defines the civic society in terms of participation at the price of socialisation but does not take a critical view of this: see 'Political Order', pp. 78–92. In more general and more critical vein, see: N. Harris, 'Beliefs in Society' (London, 1968) pp. 104–41; Anderson, in 'Towards Socialism', pp. 11–52; Mann, in 'American Sociological Review', xxxv (1970) 423–39; and Miliband, 'State in Capitalist Society', pp. 179–264.

6. Cf. P. Berger and T. Luckmann, 'The Social Construction of Reality' (London, 1967), for a more detailed discussion: pp. 65–145.

7. Cf. C. W. Mills, 'The Power Elite' (New York, 1956) passim; Miliband, 'State in Capitalist Society', pp. 146–78; Olsen, 'Logic of Collective Action', passim; G. Parry, 'Political Elites' (London, 1969) pp. 64–105.

8. On the various points and illustrations in this paragraph, see: S. Carmichael and C. V. Hamilton, 'Black Power' (Harmondsworth, 1969) and L. M. Killian, 'The Impossible Revolution' (New York, 1968); Bell (ed.), 'Radical Right', and M. P. Rogin, 'The Intellectuals and McCarthy' (Cambridge, Mass., 1967); Anderson, in 'Towards Socialism', pp. 39–40; P. Seale and M. McConville, 'French Revolution 1968' (Harmondsworth, 1968) and C. Posner (ed.), 'Reflections on the Revolution in France 1968' (Harmondsworth, 1969).

9. The Anglo-American evidence for this pattern is meticulously reviewed by Mann, in 'American Sociological Review', xxxv (1970) 423–39.

10. For the background and course of the Nazi rise to power, see: R. Dahrendorf, 'Society and Democracy in Germany' (London, 1968); E. Eyck, 'A History of the Weimar Republic', 2 vols (London, 1962–4); S. M. Lipset, 'Political Man' (London, 1959) pp. 131–52; H. D. Lasswell et al., 'World Revolutionary Elites' (Cambridge, Mass., 1965) pp. 194–318; F. Neumann, 'Behemoth' (London, 1944); E. Nolte, 'Three Faces of Fascism' (London, 1965); Parsons, 'Essays', pp. 104–23; G. Roth, 'The Social Democrats in Imperial Germany' (Englewood Cliffs, 1965); H. Rothfels, 'German Opposition to Hitler' (Chicago, 1962); D. Schoenbaum, 'Hitler's Social Revolution' (London, 1967); and S. J. Woolf (ed.), 'The Nature of Fascism' (London, 1968) and 'European Fascism' (London, 1968).

11. On the role of marginality in Germany, see: Lasswell et al., 'World Revolutionary Elites', pp. 288–99; and also Schoenbaum, 'Hitler's Social Revolution', esp. pp. 22–45.

12. This is true of actual war – peace-time military expenditure typically serves to maintain the strength of the economic centre through the resultant profits and production: see P. A. Baran and P. M. Sweezy, 'Monopoly Capital' (Harmondsworth, 1968) pp. 178–214.

13. For a discussion of 'market rationality' and 'plan rationality', see Dahrendorf, 'Essays', pp. 215–31.

14. On the *nomenklatura* system, see G. Ionescu, 'The Politics of the European Communist States' (London, 1967) pp. 60–4; for Germany, Schoenbaum, 'Hitler's Social Revolution', passim.

8 Retrospect and Prospect

1. Cf. the caustic comments of Alvin Gouldner on Parsons' concern for convergence: A. Gouldner, 'The Coming Crisis of Western Sociology' (London, 1971) pp. 17–8; also R. W. Friedrichs, 'A Sociology of Sociology' (New York, 1970) pp. 11–30 and passim.

2. For a discussion of the philosophical problems involved, see Rudner, 'Philosophy of Social Science', pp. 84–111.

3. Gurr has developed such causal models but his are concerned only with the most immediate causes of 'internal war' and not with the general structural contradictions and social processes underlying them: see 'Why Men Rebel', pp. 319–52.

4. Cf. K. Burridge, 'New Heaven, New Earth' (Oxford, 1969) pp. 4–8. Burridge provides an analysis of cargo cults that can be fitted into the model without undue strain; for a useful analysis of religious responses

to economic, social and ethical deprivation, see C. Y. Glock and R. Stark, 'Religion and Society in Tension' (Chicago, 1965) pp. 242–59.

5. Thus there is much empirical and theoretical work on subtypes such as *coups d'état*, peasant revolutions, urban riots, pre-industrial crowds, etc.; these subtypes can be specified in terms of radicalism, methods, participants, structural contexts, institutionalisation, and so on, and incorporated into the general theory.

Index